Wado-Ryu Karate
The Complete Art
Uncovered

by

Frank Johnson

www.orient-publishing.com

Dedicated to my wife Christine,
for her love and support

Designed and typeset in 11/13 Sabon by Welshpool Printing Group, Severn Farm Enterprise Park, Welshpool, Powys, SY21 7DF, UK.

Contents

Contents

Frank scoring with a Mawashigeri (Roundhouse kick) - All Japan 1978.

Foreword

Wado-Ryu Karate has been my life for the last 40 years. I have dreamt, trained and studied this great Art, sometimes feeling as if I am getting near the top of the mountain only to slip back down again.

I regard myself as having been fortunate to have studied under the great masters of Wado-Ryu, including two years in Japan. Training many times with Master Ohtsuka, the founder and a martial artist that developed a karate so unique and in-depth its boundaries are almost unlimited.

I have put all my heart and soul into the book, including many techniques I have never seen in print, also versions on kata. I do not wish to comment on which is best, I will leave that to others. In this book, and my two other books Wado-Ryu Fighting Techniques Uncovered and Wado Ryu Karate Katas Uncovered, I wish to give as complete a picture of the Art as I can. In the words of Master Ohtsuka, the secret of karate is looking for the secret. I do hope you find some secrets in this book.

Acknowledgement

I am indebted to countless people for their help with this book, and those whom I have trained with over the years. Especially my Mother and Father for all their help and support over the years; to my wife Christine, and to Sensei Kuniaki Sakagami. To my other Japanese Instructor in England, Master Tatsuo Suzuki. To my Instructors in Japan, Grand Master Hironori Ohtsuka, Master Thoru Arakawa, Master Inoue Motokatsu, Sensei Hisao Murase and Sensei Meada. Also to Gareth Ingram, 2002 Wado-Ryu Open Kata Champion of England, for his assistance with the photographs in this book.

Frank Johnson, Shropshire, England June 2005

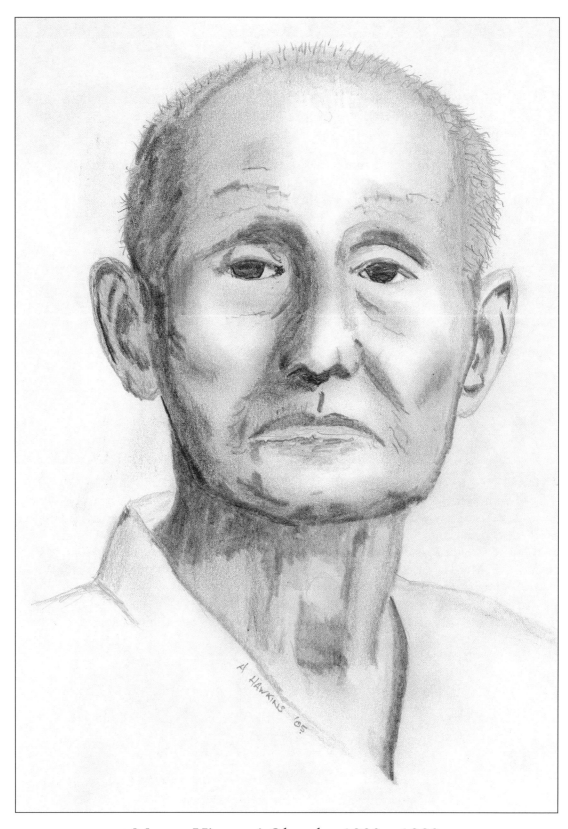

Master Hironori Ohtsuka 1892 - 1982

History of Wado-Ryu

CHRONOLOGY

1st June 1892	Hironori Ohtsuka - Born
1897	Started Ju-Jitsu - Training
1905	Started practicing Shindo -Yoshin-Ryu
1917	Began work at Kawasaki Bank
1919	Ohtsuka became master of Bone Setting
1921	Awarded Shindo-Yoshin-Ryu Ju-Jitsu graduation certificate
1922	Started practicing with Gichin Funakoshi
1928	Became Bone-setter full time
1934	Ohtsuka karate recognised as an independent style
1935	Ohtsuka becomes a full time instructor
1940	Wado-Ryu officially recognised style for the first time
1944	Ohtsuka asked to become Chief instructor for Japan by Dai-Nippon Budo-Kai.
1950's	Wado-Ryu grows fast. Also sees first karate championships
1963	Ohtsuka sent three top Karate-Ka to the West, to demonstrate Wado-Ryu; Tatsuo Suzuki, Toru Arakawa and Takashima Sensei.
1966	Ohtsuka awarded Kun-Goto-soukuo Kyoku Ju-jitsu Show from the Emperor of Japan Hirohito (for dedication to karate)
1972	Award Meijin (top title in Japan)
29th January 1982	Master Ohtsuka Meijin died.

Wado-Ryu History

The history of Wado-Ryu is somewhat of a complex affair, which is what you would expect. Master Ohsukas life spanned one of the most eventful times in history, with the first and second world wars to mention just two of the major events. Most peoples' lives in Japan would take some following.

In the 1980's I was editor of Wado-World magazine I received hundreds of articles from all over the world. I also interviewed many of the world's top Wado-Ryu instructors and talked with Master Ohtsuka himself, researching all my material and recalling the many conversions I had in Japan in the 70's. I have tried to piece the Wado-Ryu story together completely unbiased and without political infighting, I am sure that more information is out there but as old Masters die it is getting less and less reliable.

The Wado-Ryu story begins with the birth of Hironori Ohtsuka on the first of June 1892 he was the eldest son of Tokujiro Ohtsuka and his wife Sato. Ohtsuka's father was a Doctor of medicine, practicing at Shimodate City Hospital and because of this he had high social standing with a good income for the times, so he was able to look after the family well.

Ohtsuka said he was a sickly child so his mother and father decided that some kind of martial arts would build him up. In the Spring of 1897, aged 5 years old he started school and his mother's grandfather called Chorjiro Ebashi was asked to instruct him in Ju-jitsu. He was shown punching, kicking, throwing locks and vital points, Ohtsuka was to say later this got him interested in martial arts for the rest of his life.

In 1905 – he went to Shimozuma middle school, it was here that he joined the Shintoyoshin-Ryu school of Ju-jitsu under Tatsusaburo Nakayama. It is said that the founder Akiyama was at a Shinto shrine in Tenmangu when he noticed a willow tree bending with the weight of the snow on its branches and yet how it yielded to the weight of the snow thus avoiding damage. From these studies he developed a style with around three hundred movements; this style was to play a major part in later years as Ohtsuka developed the Wado-Ryu style.

In 1910 Ohtsuka went to Waseda University where he studied business, while there he continued to study other martial arts visiting many clubs mainly Ju-jitsu schools. There is a lot of speculation over which ones. In 1913 it is believed his father died and in 1917 he started work at the Kawasaki Bank.

In July of 1922 Gichin Funakoshi was invited to give a demonstration of Okinawa Karate (formally known as Tode) by the Japanese education department. Ohtsuka was impressed with the new art form and went to visit Funakoshi at the Meiseijuke (house of Okinawa students) he asked him if he would teach him all he knew about this Art of the Ryu Kyu Islands.

1925 saw the death of his mother. And in1928 he left the Kawasaki Bank to become a full time bone-setter (it seems bone setting was a common side-line learnt by top martial artists and no doubt with Ohtsuka's father being a doctor he was into healing arts). It is said that the bone-setting practice was not too successful as he was always out training or teaching martial arts, and that he neglected the business a little.

It is said that by the end of the 1920's Ohtsuka had developed quite a lot of the Wado-Ryu style of movements and he registered himself as a member of the Nippon-Kobudo-Shinko-Kai (Japanese Martial Arts Federation). It was around this time that Ohtsuka began to drift away from Funakoshi; Master Funakoshi had awarded him Dan grades. Some of his contemporaries said that Ohtsuka wanted to do more fighting. Only they knew and sadly they are no longer with us to put the record straight. Whatever reason, it seems Master Funakoshi and Ohtsuka maintained a profound mutual respect for each other. By May of 1934 Ohtsuka's karate was recognised as an independent style.

Lots of different versions of when he named the style Wado-Ryu have been put forward, I asked him myself in 1977, when did he think of the name, his reply was sometime in the 1930's but could not remember the exact date. In 1938 he first thought of calling it Shinshu-Wado-Ryu a sort of patriotic name for Japan. But in the light on the times building up to the second world war you can quite understand why he may have considered this, in any case two years later just the words Wado-Ryu were registered. It is interesting to note that at a major demonstration in Kyoto on the 5th of May 1940 the words Wado-Ryu were used in the programme. The war years were a bad time for all kinds of martial arts, with many top students losing their lives. In 1944 the Dai Nippon Budo-Kai asked him to become chief instructor of karate for Japan.

When the war ended in 1945 martial arts were forbidden, Ohtsuka continued to practice and teach in private, a lot of clubs pretended to be doing boxing to get round the ban.

In the 1950's karate was allowed again and Wado-Ryu prospered in its popularity. Firstly it was mainly in Universities, then small private clubs, little by little they began to grow in number. In the middle to late 1950's competitions began to get more popular.

The 1960's saw Wado-Ryu gain popularity overseas, in 1963 Ohtsuka sent a three man team to do major demonstrations in the U.S.A and Europe comprising, Tatsuo Suzuki, Toru Arakawa and Takashima Sensei. Tatsuo Suzuki has been a major force in bringing Wado- Ryu to many students outside Japan.

In 1966 Ohtsuka was awarded Kun-Goto-soukuo Kyoku Ju jitsu Show from the Emperor of Japan Hirohito for his dedication to karate, and in 1972 he was awarded Meijin the ultimate title in martial arts. Ohtsuka continued to practice and perform demonstrations almost up to his death. He died on the 29th of January 1982.

How to study the book

- All pictures are taken from the front.

- To give readers a better idea of foot positions the floor has been left in on all photographs.

- To enable the reader to readily distinguish the right and left movements in the photographs, where appropriate Frank wears a white band on his right hand.

- Once you understand the way the book is laid out you will be able to find a specific movement from a Kata etc easily.

- The Kiai K (shout) for Katas are placed at the traditional points.

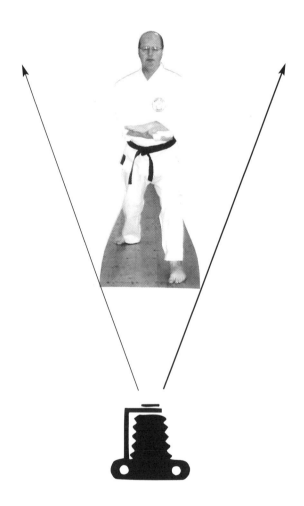

ETIQUETTE

Etiquette is a very important part of traditional Japanese Karate, here I show you the way of bowing taught to me. Methods vary from club to club depending on your instructor.

When you bow the feeling you get should be one of inner calm and should be done in a dignified manner.

Stand upright, feet apart in Musubi-Dachi stance.

Kneel down with right knee keeping hands on front of thigh.

Bow from waist bringing hands together. Keep your eyes forward at all times

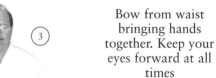

Insteps flat on floor and back straight.

Back to upright position.

Get up by sliding out left leg then bringing right leg to left. Back into Musubi-Dachi position 1, finally do standing bow Tachi-Rei.

Tachi-Rei standing bow

MOKUSO and ZA-ZEN

Mokuso (Empty Mind Training) and Za-Zen (Seated Meditation) is for a Karate-Ka (person that practices Karate) very important.

It would be true to say that if two people are in combat of the same or similar skill, the persons mind is going to play a major factor in who wins and who loses. Mokuso is usually done while sitting on your knees with your bottom resting on heels and instep flat on floor.

The idea is to try and rid your mind of all conscious thought, a good start is to count one to ten only thinking of counting, then after a lot of practise try thinking of nothing at all. You will find to start with it will be very difficult. If you can do 5 minutes to start you are doing well.

Western students find sitting on their knees difficult, so you may like to try Za-Zen (photo above). Keep your back straight, legs crossed, hands resting on the front of your legs, thumbs just touching. Try to breath slowly, staying calm and relaxed. Remember having a calm mind when sparring will help you.

WARMING-UP EXERCISES

Karate involves the use of all parts of the body, so it is essential to warm up before training to avoid injury. As most readers of this book will already be doing Wado-Ryu Karate I have only included a small selection of warming-up exercises.

Rub your knees to warm them up.

Bend at knees, back straight, then back to photo one.

With your left leg straight gently push down with hand.

Keeping your back straight, lower your hips trying to keep back leg straight.

Go even further than photo 4. Still try to keep back straight.

Crouch down, leg straight as you can.

Sit upright with soles of feet together, feet drawn into your groin as much as you can.

(8) Sit on floor, gradually try to spread your legs as wide as you can.

Bend forward to stretch your inner thighs.

(9)

Twist body to side, grab ankle and pull yourself down towards your foot.

(10)

Twist body sideways and again pull yourself down towards foot.

(11)

Both 10, 11, 12 & 13 should be repeated both sides.

(12)

Bring leg up to groin keeping other leg straight and stretch forward.

(13)

Cross your leg over the other one and place arm behind knee and twist backwards as far as you can.

(14)

14b

Sit on floor, tuck legs behind you. Push your body upwards, this will stretch the front of your legs.

Swing your arms around in a circle.

Cross your one arm across body, place other arm just above elbow joint and pull in looking the same way as pulling arm.

Place hands together and push hard against each other.

Place you arm behind head and other arm on elbow, pull backwards and down.

PARTNER WORK

There are many exercises for partners, here are two to get you started.

Place leg on shoulders and bring head towards leg.

Hold hands, knees together and keeping back straight lower yourself down.

MAKIWARA TRAINING

Makiwara Training is good for correct punching, strengthening your wrists and increasing your punching power, especially for Gyakuzuki. The question we need to ask is, in these modern times should we still be practicing on the Makiwara? There is some evidence that suggests that you may develop arthritis in your hands in later years from over-training on the Makiwara. Only you can make the decision as to whether you want to take the risk or not. Having said that training on a Makiwara can give your punches more focus and power.

How to make a Makiwara

You need a length of wood 5-6 feet (155cm) long. About 5ins (12cm) wide at the base, tapering to approx 1$\frac{1}{2}$ ins (4cm) at the top, so that you have some movement when you hit the Makiwara.

Dig a hole in the ground and concrete the Makawara in so that it is approximately chest height. Tie around the top some form of padding, traditionally straw was used. I use some hard rubber, and cover it with hardwearing fabric, which you change when worn through.

How to punch

You can use any punch on the Makiwara, but the main ones used are: Gyakuzuki, Uraken. For Gyakuzuki start with your forward arm in Gedan-Barai, weight on your back foot, transfer weight to your forward foot as you punch, twisting your hips pulling back the Gedan-Barai onto your hip.

For back-fist stand more to the side of the Makiwara, twist your hips in the same direction as the striking fist (photos on page 21-22 clearly show these movements as they are performed).

It is not uncommon to take the skin off your knuckles when you first start. The skin on your knuckles becomes callous and hard. Take care and stop immediately if you feel; anything is wrong.

TETSU-GETA (Iron Clogs)

Tetsu-Geta is the old method of training to build up your leg muscles. You only need one as using two at a time can cause you to twist your knee on the non-kicking leg. Ensure you warm-up first to avoid injury and muscle strains. 10-15 kicks to start with on each leg, building up to 30-40. Do not over do it to start with, it will take many months to build up your leg muscles. **YOUNG PEOPLE STILL GROWING SHOULD NOT DO TETSU-GETA TRAINING.**

There are a number of different Geta used. Some have a thong that goes between the toes. The one I use, given to me whilst I was in Japan, allows you to bend your toes when kicking front kick etc, so you can use the exact muscles. It has 4 slots to thread the Karate belt through so as to make it impossible to come off the foot when tied securely around the ankle (see photo on page 23). The weight should not be too heavy for you, the one I use is about 6lb (3kg).

HAND WEIGHT

A small metal hand weight is an invaluable tool for helping you build speed into your punches. It should fit comfortable into your hand (see photos on page 25) so that you can punch easily. Punching with this weight will give you a good 'snap-back' action and increased hand strength and speed.

WADO-RYU

WA = Harmony/peace

DO = Way

RYU = Style

FIST = Strength/strong/powerful

DOVE/BIRD = Often seen in Japanese Culture

Stand in front of Makiwara, body weight on back foot, twist your body to front as you punch. Transfer your weight onto forward leg.

Stand to the side of Makiwara, twist your hips hitting Makiwara with back of knuckles.

Tie the Karate belt tight, stop immediately if it starts to come undone.

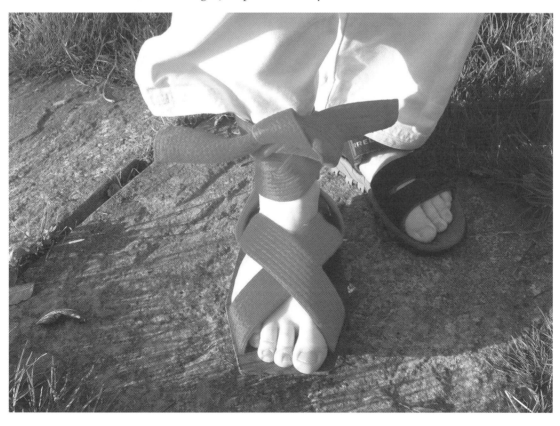

Frank (above) practising Mawashigeri and (below) Maegeri using Gata.

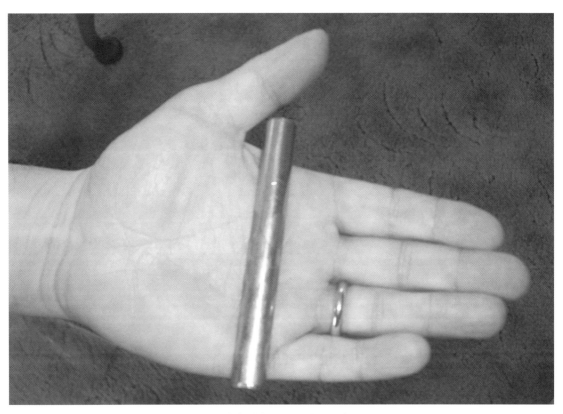

Frank holding hand weights.

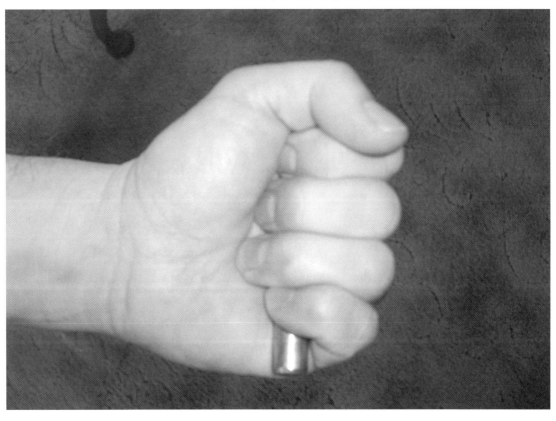

BASIC HAND-FEET

It would be true to say that it takes a few years to build up the strength in your hands and feet to be able to deliver a strong punch or kick. You need to practice getting your hands and feet into the correct form so that you can do it without thinking.

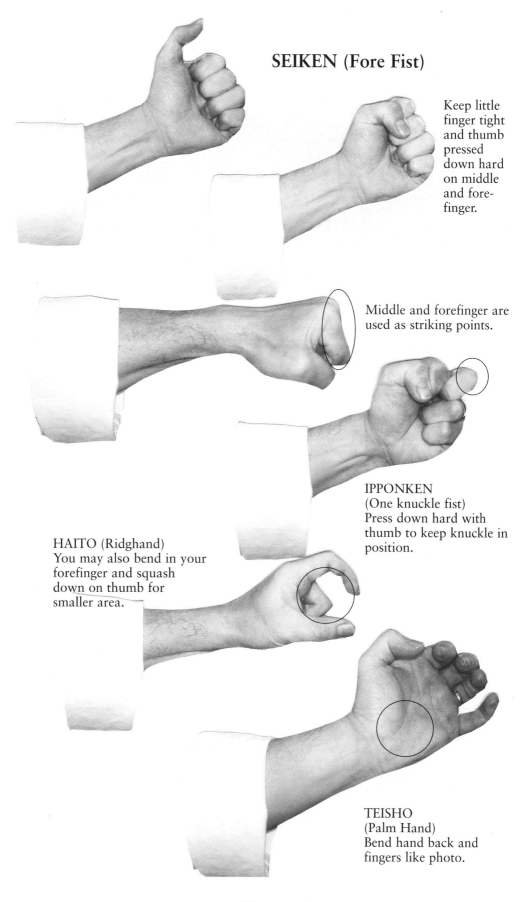

SEIKEN (Fore Fist)

Keep little finger tight and thumb pressed down hard on middle and fore-finger.

Middle and forefinger are used as striking points.

IPPONKEN
(One knuckle fist)
Press down hard with thumb to keep knuckle in position.

HAITO (Ridghand)
You may also bend in your forefinger and squash down on thumb for smaller area.

TEISHO
(Palm Hand)
Bend hand back and fingers like photo.

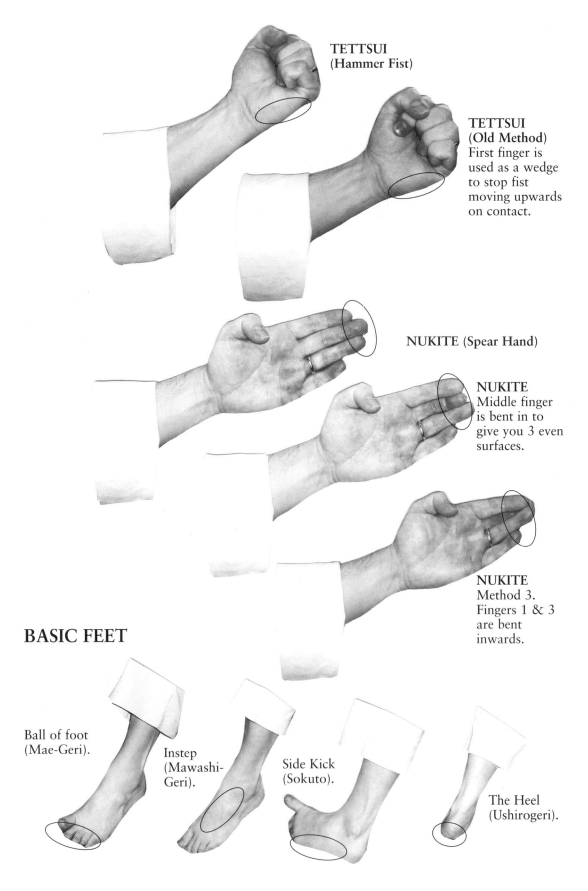

TETTSUI
(Hammer Fist)

TETTSUI
(Old Method)
First finger is
used as a wedge
to stop fist
moving upwards
on contact.

NUKITE (Spear Hand)

NUKITE
Middle finger
is bent in to
give you 3 even
surfaces.

NUKITE
Method 3.
Fingers 1 & 3
are bent
inwards.

BASIC FEET

Ball of foot
(Mae-Geri).

Instep
(Mawashi-
Geri).

Side Kick
(Sokuto).

The Heel
(Ushirogeri).

28

KIHON
(Basics)

Basic techniques are most important if students wish to reach a high level in Karate. They mould your body and build your spirit, you can never do too many! Within Kihon is correct form, how to relax, correct balance, correct leg, hips and wrist movement. Building power of technique and mental strength. There is an old saying that if the foundations of your house are weak your house will fall down, if the foundations of your Karate are weak you will be knocked down.

BASIC PUNCH

Starting from Kiba-Dachi stance (Naihanchi).

Punch out with your left arm, your punch should try to brush your suit as it goes past, keeping as tight as you can without over-reaching yourself.

Pull back other arm at same time. Twisting arm and fist over simultaneously.

Try to keep your shoulders relaxed.

Do not twist your fist until the last split second.

JUNZUKI
(Forward Punch)

Junzuki is a step forward movement.
Keep hips down, shifting body weight
from rear to front leg, pull arm back
as you punch with opposite arm.

KETTE-JUNZUKI

Kick Maegeri with rear leg under your
forward arm, then step down with your
kicking leg, punching Junzuki into no 2
photo.

GYAKUZUKI
(Reverse Punch)

Using a semi-circular action bring your rear leg around, punching into next stance. A nice flowing action is required.

KETTE-GYAKUZUKI

Kick Maegeri with back leg, step down into Gyakuzuki stance.

Side View

GYAKUZUKI-NO-TSUKKOMI
(Forward Leaning Reverse Punch)

Keeping your body from rising too high use a nice flowing action when moving forward. Around 70% of your weight is on your forward leg.

KETTE-GYAKUZUKI-NO-TSUKKOMI
(Kick and Forward Leaning Punch)

Kick Maegeri under forward arm with back leg. Try not to come up too much with your body, try to end up as in photo 3.

JUNZUKI-NO-TSUKKOMI
(Forward Leaning Punch)

Step forward as you lean from the waist punching to the face.

KETTE-JUNZUKI-NO-TSUKKOMI

Kick with back leg Maegeri then into same stance as photo 3.

TOBIKOMIZUKI
(Snap Back Punch)

Slide left foot forward at same time bringing up both fists and punch with left, right going on to your chest. Snap back arm as in photo 4.

Start from photo 1 stance Hidari-Shizentai

Bring right foot up half way and left foot back half way into photo 1.

NAGASHIZUKI
(Sweeping Away Punch)

From Hidari Shizentai slide forward with left leg, bring up both fists punching with left arm. Your back foot moves across. Snap back your left arm, move right foot up and left foot back into Hidari Shizentai.

Back View of
photo 3

Nagashizuki is one of the best fighting moves and in the fighting section of the book I have included a number of techniques just on this movement.

34

MAEGERI (Front Kick)

Start by bringing your knee straight up, keeping toes back. Keep non-kicking foot flat on the floor, snap kick back to photo 2 before putting foot on floor.

SOKUTO (Side Kick)

Start by bringing your knee straight up, then twist your hips keeping your arms close to your body. Non-kicking foot flat on floor. After kick, pull back leg inwards like photo 3 to protect your groin before putting back onto floor.

USHIRO-GERI
(Back Kick)

From left fighting stance step across with forward leg. Kick backwards with your right foot, using your heel as striking point. After kick, step down into right stance.

MAWASHI-GERI
(Round Kick)

From left fighting stance bring your knee straight up.

NIDAN-GERI
(Flying Double Kick)

Begin to twist hips as you whip your leg around. As soon as you complete the kick snap kick back to photo 1. Keep your hands close to body and back leg bent, foot flat on the floor.

Starting from fighting stance throw your back leg upwards to get height, then kick front kick when in the air, landing back into same stance. Generally speaking Tobi-Maegeri means one kick but most instructors call it Nidan-Geri.

UKE-WAZA
(Blocking Techniques)

The best blocking technique is not to do one, but move your body into a position where you can counter attack. But this is not always possible, so we need to learn how to block. Within the book there are many blocking techniques, the following pages show the main ones used. Always use your bodies natural turning or twisting the hips to give you help in the block, not just arm movement.

MAWATTE
(Turning)

I would think that I am on safe ground to say almost everyone that starts Karate finds turning difficult. Photo no 1 shows how your back foot moves across as you get ready to turn. Do not turn too soon as you want to get the acceleration of your body to help give power into your block. Mawatte is used a great deal, so master it well.

Do not turn until your foot is fully across.

MAWATTE GEDAN-BARAI
(Lower Block)

On turning bring your fist up to your lower shoulder and sweep it across the body.

MAWATTE JODAN-UKE
(Head Block)

On turning bring your arm up and across your face, twisting your arm as you go.

38

MAHANMI-NO-NEKOASHI
(Side-viewing cat stance)

Step forward to perform block, as you move your blocking hand comes near the side of your head. At this point your body is facing forward.

Front View
A split
second
before block
is done.

Side View
Halfway into forward movement.

You now need to twist your body away from blocking hand to get power into the block, but do not over do it. Keep control of your body.

View at end of block.

Note:
Shuto-Uke block is used extensively in Katas, accompanied by the Mahanmi-No-Nekoashi stance.

40%

60%

Mahanmi-no-Nekoashi is one of the most difficult moves to do in Wado-Ryu Karate when performing Shuto-Uke Jodan at the same time, Master Ohtsuka founder of Wado-Ryu told me that 20 years would not be long enough to learn this move.

BLOCKING SOTO-UKE
& UCHI-UKE
(Outside & Inside Block respectively)

Bring your arm across body, block with outside of wrist.

Soto-Uke

Bring your arm across your body blocking with the inside of the wrist.

Uchi-Uke

OTHER STANCES USED IN THIS BOOK

% denotes weight on each leg.

GYAKU-NEKOASHI (Reverse cat stance)

MASHOMEN-NO-NEKOASHI (Front view stance)

HEISOKUDACHI (Closed Stance)

50%   50%

80%   20%

90%   10%

SEISHAN-DACHI (Even Stance)

NAIHANCHI (Even Stance)

The distancing between legs vary to some degree by the length of your leg. To say it is so many fists, or so many inches, or millimetres would be to do a dis-service to the reader. Your own training and instructor will put you on the right track.

50%   50%

50%   50%

SHIKO-DACHI (Even Stance)

KOKUTSUDACHI (Back Stance)

60%

40%

50%   50%

41

SPEED & REFLEX TRAINING

It is said that the average first Dan's reflexes are twice as quick as the average person. Included in this small section are some tips on training, to get you up to speed.

Relaxation greatly improves your speed and reflexes so always try and relax when practicing.

Figure 1 shows you how to practice to improve your hand and eye co-ordination. One partner holds their open hands up, the idea is they move one hand in any order forward or back approx 6 ins (15cms). The punching partner must react instantly, punching the moving hand (with control), followed by their other hand punching to the body (see photo 2).

Move left or right to avoid punch.

After practice you will be able to hit the hand almost before they have moved it. Photo 3 shows Frank moving his body to the side, this is good practice for reflexes when his partner standing in same as photo 1 punches to the face with either left or right arm. Photo 4 shows practicing for quick pull-back of the arm. Partner stands in front, open hands at waist level on outside of body, as other partner punches to the body you do a clapping action. The aim is to touch the body and pull back before the hands come together. Photo 4 shows movement that has not succeeded in pulling back in time.

KIHON GUMITE
(Basic Sparring)

One of the most important aspects of Wado-Ryu is incorporated into Kihon-Gumite, that is Ten-i, Ten-Tai, Ten-Gi, which means change or move position, or to twist or change form, to change or execute a technique. Kihon-Gumite uses these movements to the maximum, the student is trying to avoid the greater force with the least force they can and as fast as they can without losing form and technique.

CORRECT DISTANCING

1. All Kihon Kumite start from Musubi-dachi stance. It cannot be stressed enough how important the correct distancing is in Kihon, and all fighting moves. Distancing is learnt through experience but approximately two arms lengths apart at the beginning is a good start.

2. Bow Tachi-rei keeping your eyes on your opponents eyes at all times.

3. Defender 3A steps back away from attacker. Attacker 3B steps forwards. All Kihon-Kumite has the defender going back and the attacker going forward.

KIHON KUMITE No 1

1. Defender steps back into right stance, attacker forward into right stance, attacker punches to face with right arm.

2. Move your whole body to the right to avoid punch and block with your right arm.

Defenders feet should be equally balanced.

3. Attacker punches Gyakuzuki, defender twists hips 180° to avoid the punch, and counters with upward punch to the body.

4. After punch move away in opposite direction back to Fig. 3 page 44.

KIHON KUMITE
No 2

1. Defender steps back into right, attacker forward in right. Attacker punches with right arm to face.

2. Move all your body to the right same as Kihon No 1 photo 2.

Note: Like Kihon 1 your blocking arm uses the right side of arm for block.

3. Attacker kicks Sokuto to body with right leg, move body to right and block with right arm (see photo 4).

KIHON KUMITE No 2

4. Defender keep your body down, in all the Kihons. The defenders unused arm is kept approximately on the body around the middle of the solar plexus. It is important your right arm is not straight to give you good cover on the block.

Reverse of 5

5 & 6. Move back into your attacker immediately and counter-attack with Haito right hand and Teisho to liver and kidneys. Attacker moves around to his left, defender moving back.

KIHON KUMITE No 3

1. Defender steps back into right stance, attacker forward into right stance. Attacker punches to face with right arm, defender blocks same as Kihon No 1 photo 2.

2. Attacker kicks Maegeri (front kick) to body. Defender moves back in striking ipponken to solar plexus with right fist in an upward direction and striking the inside of attackers left leg with ipponken - left fist.

3. Attacker moves back into right stance. Defender moves left leg back first staying in right stance. Back to photo 1 page 44.

KIHON KUMITE No 4

1. Defender steps back into right stance, attacker forward into left stance, attacker punches to face with left arm. See photo 2 Kihon Kumite No 1.

2. Attacker punches right Gyakuzuki to face, move body to right and leans backwards sweeping punch away with hand.

3. Use the momentum of your body as you go back in. Cover attackers punch with left arm and strike Ipponken to side of body below the arm.

3a. Attacker moves back into left stance. Defender moves right foot back first as you move away. Back to photo 1 page 44.

KIHON KUMITE No 5

1. Defender steps back into right stance, attacker forward into left stance and punches to face with left arm. Block same as photo 2 Kihon Kumite No 1.

2. Block down with right hand as simultaneously you bring your left arm up preparing to grip waist.

3. Move in and hit under the nose with Ipponken or Haito.

4. Move in and elbow under arm.

Reverse of No 4

4a. Note you still have hold of punching arm.

KIHON KUMITE No 5

5. Pull your right foot back to your left, off-balancing your attacker slightly. Your elbow going under his arm. Move left foot round so as to throw him onto the ground. Keep tight hold of his arm.

6. Making a lock on the arm (study the photo to see the hand position).

Reverse of No 5

7. Keeping control of your attacker place your right knee on to his arm and push arm down towards floor.

8. Punch him in face with right hand.

9. Keeping control of your attacker place your right arm on to his arm and push arm down towards floor.

10. Attacker rolls over to his left.

11. Stand up together.

Reverse of 8

Side view of 9

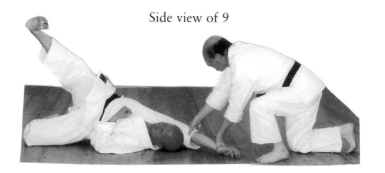

KIHON KUMITE No 6

1. Defender steps back into right stance, attacker forward into left stance. Attacker punches to face with left arm, block same as Kihon No 1 photo 2.

2. Attacker steps up with back foot and kicks Sokuto to body. Block same as Kihon No 2

3. Attacker then punches to face Gyakuzuki. Using same movement as Kihon No 1 with your feet. Block with open right hand and punch into side of body, move away defender into right, attacker in left stances.

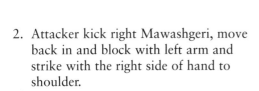

KIHON KUMITE No 7

1. Defender steps back into right, attacker forward into left stance. Attacker punches to face with left arm. Block same as Kihon No 1 photo 2.

2. Attacker kick right Mawashgeri, move back in and block with left arm and strike with the right side of hand to shoulder.

3. 2nd version - Attacker using front kick and defender is striking on side of neck.

Forward view of block and strike.

KIHON KUMITE No 8

1. Defender steps back into right stance, attacker into right, attacker punches off front hand to body, defender moves their body to right and block with the forward arm. Defenders stance is Tate-Seishan.

2. Attacker punches left Gyakuzuki to face. Move your left foot to side and block up using your forearm.
Note: Some instructors teach blocking with elbow.

3. Move back in and punch to thigh using Ipponken.

3a. Reverse of 3.

4. Defender moves his right foot more into Shiko-Dachi stance and drives elbow into body. Left hand reinforcing the elbow.

4a

Reverse of 4

5. Twisting your body to left with both hands on attackers left arm. Pull his right leg forward a little with your right knee to overbalance him. Then push him away as you go back into right stance. Defender back into right stance.

5a

Note: 5 is done with a quick pace and should only overbalance him a little way.

KIHON KUMITE No 9

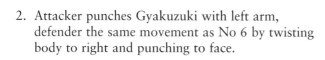

1. Defender and attacker same as No 8.

2. Attacker punches Gyakuzuki with left arm, defender the same movement as No 6 by twisting body to right and punching to face.

Note: Some instructors teach punch to body.

3. The Gyakuzuki is aimed for the right side of the defenders chest, high up near the shoulder. Defender brings around left leg back into right stance and attacker moves back into right stance.

KIHON KUMITE No 10

1. Both attacker and defender in right stance. Attacker punches to face, defender blocks with side of open hand.

2. Attacker then punches left Gyakuzuki to face, move inside the punch, cover it with your right hand at the same time your left arm covers the attackers right arm.

3. Move in more, gripping the suit with right arm and doing elbow to body. Push his Gyakuzuki arm up with your right elbow.

4. At the same time move your right foot to the right and with the flat of your hand strike upward to groin.

5. Twist your body around and inwards to attackers body keeping a tight grip with right hand. You need to be very close, your left hand is on attacking back leg and is going to push upwards as you pull hard with right arm downwards, throwing attacker straight over.

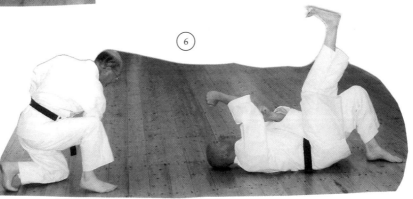

6. Your attacker will land on their back.

7. After, attacker rolls over to his left. As defender moves right foot to right, stand up feet together in Musubidachi stance.

JIYU-GUMITE
(Free Fighting)

Jiyu-Gumite uses all your training to its full effect, it is the nearest as a Karate-Ka (person that practices Karate) we come to real combat. Great skill is required to control the techniques during Jiyu-Gumite, it is such a wide subject I cannot do it justice in these pages, so I also direct the readers to my book Wado-Ryu Fighting Techniques Uncovered for an indepth study of this part of the Art.

CORRECT DISTANCING

You can never reach a high level in Karate without correct distancing. The aim when you attack or defend is always to hit your target. Failure to do so leaves you open to defeat. To gauge your distance will depend on your height, reach and on your reflexes and bravery. In staying close when necessary, it would be true to say only training and many sparring sessions give you this. A general rule of thumb is that you should be at least two arms lengths apart, or one step kick apart. If your attacker comes within the limits of this consider the attack already started, the speed of Wado-Ryu is such that you can blink and get hit, as by the time you open your eyes the move is too close to do anything about it! Correct distancing will help get over this problem as it will give you just a split second longer to react to attack.

Yoi Stance

Yoi stance is one of the key stances in Wado-Ryu, often overlooked by students. You are in this stance before sparring begins and therefore your mind should be one of calm but aware of your surroundings.

Yoi stance

50% weight on each leg, both hands centre line of body.

Traditional Wado-Ryu fighting stance

Inasu

1. Counter attacking simultaneously.
2. Attacking as your opponent starts attack.

Attacker punches Gyakuzuki to face, lean your body away, blocking with back of hand, punching off the front hand to face or body.

Attacker punches to body Gyakuzuki, keep body more upright, punching off front hand. Both photos 1-2 uses attackers momentum to give defender more power.

Attacker punches to face. Use your forward hand to sweep punch away, leaning back a little. Counter with right Gyakuzuki.

Attacker punches Gyakuzuki. Move your body a little to the right, sweeping your arm down to block. This is one of the best blocks for Gyakuzuki to the body. Counter with right Gyakuzuki.

(5) Attacker punches Gyakuzuki to face, move your body weight on to right leg and head to side a little, counter with left Gyakuzuki.

(6) Attacker punches to face. Move body to side punch over top of incoming punch.

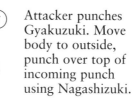

(7) Attacker punches Gyakuzuki. Move body to outside, punch over top of incoming punch using Nagashizuki.

(8)

Sen

As attacker starts move, simultaneously you attack hitting a split second before attacker. This is called Sen.

Attacker punches to face. Be brave and move in, blocking with back hand and punch off front hand.

Attacker punches to face, step to your right and hit attacker with Teisho.

Attacker punches Gyakuzuki to face, lean to right and strike Uraken into stomach (back of hand).

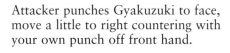

Twist your body back to left punching into stomach at same time, covering attackers non-punching hand.

Attacker punches Gyakuzuki to face, move a little to right countering with your own punch off front hand.

12a

Attacker punches Gyakuzuki to body, strike to body with your fist. Your body is sideways on in Shiko-Dachi stance, left arm covers attackers punch.

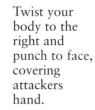

12a

Twist your body to the right and punch to face, covering attackers hand.

13

Attacker tries to punch Gyakuzuki, sensing the move you pin the arm to the body. Sensing a move is called **SEN-SEN-NO-SEN**.

Attacker punches right Gyakuzuki, twist body into Shiko-Dachi, strike side of fist into body, right hand covers.

14

SEN-SEN-NO-SEN

Sensing your attackers move, the instant it comes into their mind. You may feel this is not possible, take it from me it is!

15a

Attacker punches right Gyakuzuki to body. Twist body to the right in same movement as Kihon No 1 counter to body.

Attacker punches off front hand to body.

15b

Block attackers punch like Kihon No 1.

16a

16b

NAGASU
(flowing movement or evasion)

It is better to get a nice flowing movement when counter attacking than a jagged technique.

(1) Attacker punches towards face. Block with your back hand as you lean away a little, come back in and punch into floating ribs with Tata-Zuki (do not twist fist).

(2)

(3)

Get your left arm onto the top of arm off balancing them a little and punch again into side of body.

(1) Move in and grab arm.

(2)

Punch into side of body with Gyakuzuki.

As attacker punches Gyakuzuki, move a little inside the punch, cover with left elbow, then counter with same arm to face.

As attacker punches Gyakuzuki move a little inside his arm block Gedan-Barai.

Move forward and with left arm cover as you counter with your own body punch.

Attacker kicks front kick. Move your body inside kick (do not move too much, just a little). Keep movement going forward and punch to face, covering attackers hand.

Note: Frank's left leg close to attackers leg to stop him kicking Frank. You can also off-balance your attacker by pushing to his right.

Attacker punches Gyakuzuki. Move to the outside of his body and do Haito to solar plexus.

If you are fast you can get sideways in to your attacker, this gives you many ways to over balance them. Here Frank has come back in and his knee pushes against the attackers knee, he punches with right hand covering attackers non punching hand, pushing from here will make attacker go off balance.

ATTACKING FRONT HAND

Slap his hand to side just prior to attack.

Attack elbow joint with Tettsui back fist.

Punch Gyakuzuki to top muscle of arm to take arm out of action.

You always have a problem of how to get past the defenders front guard. Here are 4 ways to do it.

Note: Study striking points chart to give you help in all attacking moves.

Hit the back of the forward hand with Ippon-Ken (one knuckle fist)

Attacker kicks front kick. Twist your body and slap his leg to side with flat of hand. As soon as he steps down pull his foot further forward with your foot.

Twist round and keeping low, knock the front foot off the ground.

As attacker falls punch to face.

Attacker punches Gyakuzuki. Stop him in his tracks with the flat of your hand.

Move in and do Tettsui to face.

Attacker punches Gyakuzuki, defender moves his body back just a little and attacks back with his own Gyakuzuki before they can defend. Following up with back fist to face.

Front kick to inside of leg knee/muscle.

Kicking Attacks

It is difficult to do defence moves with kicks in this section. I have shown only four that I feel will give you good service. The speed of Wado-Ryu is such that kicks are best used as an attacking move.

As attacker performs Gyakuzuki drive front kick into body.

When in a little close kick back leg/knee or muscle.

Attacker punches Gyakuzuki, lean back and drive side kick into body off front leg. This will stop him for a split second giving time to counter attack.

The same move can be used for front kick, off front leg to groin.

Kick to shin is an effective way of opening up the opponent for a second move.
(Frank practices this move by kicking the Makiwara at the bottom of the wood).

Step in and kick Sokuto under arm to floating ribs.

Move your body to the side of your opponent and kick roundhouse (Mawashi-Geri) to body.

Side kick (Sokuto) to side of knee. You need to be at an angle to opponent to get the best results.

As attacker brings knee up kick down with sole of foot to block move.

Side kick to back leg as you are very close in on this, make sure you keep your guard up.

Move out to side kicking Mawashi-Geri, attacker performs Gyakuzuki.

Step out to guard side of attacker and do round house kick Mawashi-Geri to groin.

I have used only fighting moves that I have found and seen working successfully in these pages. In my book Wado-Ryu Fighting Techniques Uncovered I have gone into this part of the art in greater detail.

The art of Atemi-waza, or striking points go back many hundreds of years. They represent points on the human body that can help in disabling an attacker more effectively, you need to be accurate when hitting these points so it would be true to say a good deal of training is required. Including with the chart is a list of Wado-Ryu hand and foot moves you could use. A top grade karate-ka should be able to strike any part of the body and stop their opponent on the spot.

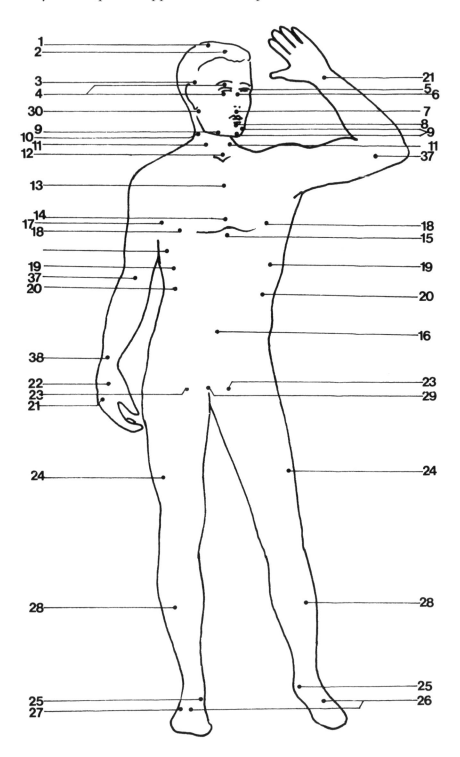

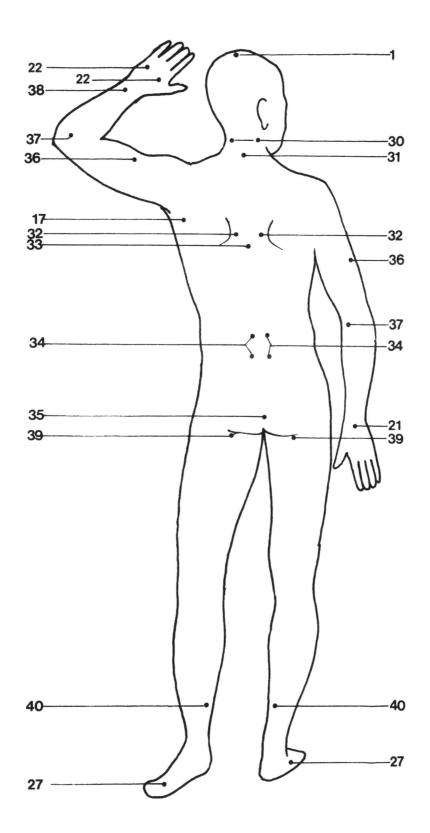

22
22
38
37
36
17
32
33
34
35
39
40
27

1
30
31
32
36
37
34
21
39
40
27

YOU SHOULD TAKE GREAT CARE WITH THESE MOVES AND NEVER STRIKE ANYONE EVEN IN FUN OR PRACTICE. THEY ARE IN THIS BOOK AS A GUIDE ONLY.

1. Centre of skull ....Elbow, bottom fist
2. Just below centre of skull.........................Head, bottom fist, elbow
3. Temples ....Back fist, one knuckle fist
4. Above and below the eyes ....Fore fist, one knuckle fist, back fist
5. Eyeballs ....Spear hand
6. Bridge of nose ....Fore fist, back fist, head, bottom fist
7. Below nose..Fore fist, back fist, one knuckle fist
8. Below mouth ....Side of hand, fore fist, one knuckle fist
9. Around the jaw ....Back fist, fore fist, knee, head, round kick
10. Side of neck ....Side of hand, round kick
11. Side of throat ....Side of hand, fore fist, bottom fist
12. Bone below wind pipe ....Bottom fist, back fist
13. Middle of chest ....Fore fist, elbow, front kick
14. Just above solar plexus............................Fore fist, elbow, front kick
15. Solar plexus   Fore fist, elbow, front kick, spear hand, knee, round kick, back kick, one knuckle fist, palm heal
16. Below the navel ....See 15
17. Under arm pit ....One knuckle fist, elbow, bottom fist
18. Under the heart ....See 15
19. In line of solar plexus...............................See 15
20. Just above navel on both sides of body ....See 15
21. Wrist ....One knuckle fist
22. Back of hand ....One knuckle fist
23. Side of groin...Front kick, knee, round kick
24. Top of leg...One knuckle fist, side kick
25. Shin bone ....Side kick, front kick, stamp kick
26. Top of foot..Stamp kick
27. Side of foot ....Stamp kick, front kick
28. Top of shin bone (front)...........................Front kick, side kick
29. Groin ....Front kick, knee, back kick
30. Back of ear..One knuckle fist, spear hand
31. Back of neck ....Bottom fist, elbow, side hand
32. Between the shoulder blades ....Front kick, fore fist, bottom fist
33. Spinal cord..See 32
34. Kidneys ....Front kick, round kick, fore fist
35. Base of spine ....Knee, front kick
36. Top of arm..One knuckle fist, fore fist
37. Elbow...Front kick, one knuckle fist
38. Wrist top ....One knuckle fist
39. Top of leg at back ....Front kick, side kick
40. Calf ....Front kick, side kick, round kick.

*Note: Stamp kick denotes side kick but in a downward direction.

TANTO-DORI
(Knife Defence)

Tanto-Dori is one of the arts Wado-Ryu excels at. You should practice with a wooden or rubber knife to start, always take into account the extra distancing for the knife. Traditionally the defender is always in right stance at the start of the attack, their heart furthest away from the knife.

Defender starting from right stance, as attacker thrusts knife at the stomach, step back and block with left forearm to the side.

Grab attackers wrist and with left fist do Uraken to face.

Move forward and elbow to the face still keeping hold of wrist.

Straighten your arm under the chin, pushing back the head, keep pulling the arm you are holding, tight against your chest.

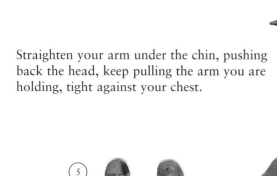

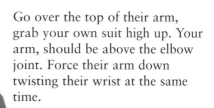

Go over the top of their arm, grab your own suit high up. Your arm, should be above the elbow joint. Force their arm down twisting their wrist at the same time.

To move away place left arm behind attackers arm pushing it away as you step back with left leg.

The attacker tries to knife the defender from right to left. Defender in right stance leaning back to avoid knife.

Step in as attacker comes back. Defender blocks arm with left arm and moves up behind attacker. Right hand on chin pull backwards, your left arm on the shoulder below right hand using it as leverage.

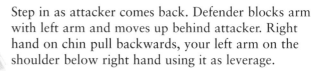

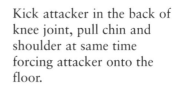

Kick attacker in the back of knee joint, pull chin and shoulder at same time forcing attacker onto the floor.

Back view of 4

⑤

Side View

Punch to face with Gyakuzuki dropping your body weight to give you more power.

Using two hands for photo 2 may also help if attacker is very powerful.

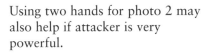

The attacker does downward knife move. Move your body back and to the side from right to left stance, lifting arm up.

Grab wrist and punch Gyakuzuki to face, keeping your left hand still holding the attackers wrist.

Kick Mawashi-Geri to body at the same time twisting attackers wrist to the left.

Keep twisting wrist as you put your right leg behind their forward leg.

As they hit the ground keep hold of the wrist and pull arm upwards.

Put your knee onto the attackers arm and push it down while kneeling on the arm, to control the knife arm. You will find you can easily take the knife from this point.

2nd DOWNWARD DEFENCE

This is almost the same as the first one but more whipping action is used by stepping more to the right.

Step across more with the right foot, turn fast to the left to whip him down.

Same as 6 & 7.

Attacker lunges knife to body with right hand.

Defender blocks with outside of arm and wrist.

*Note how Frank's body is kept away from the knife.

Grab wrist with left hand, fingers on top, at same time strike Uraken to face.

As soon as punch has hit, grab top of wrist with same hand.

4

Whip attacker round pulling arm up and pushing your knee into the elbow.

5

Keep pulling arm upwards. Stamp on the side of the face as you put your left leg over to the side of their head.

6

Fall backward trapping their arm between your two legs, this will cause great pain making it easy to take the knife from the attacker.

Attacker lunges right, knife to body. Drop down at very last second and kick to groin off front foot.

Punch with right hand to lower stomach or even groin, then do two palm heels to stomach and back.

Come straight up under chin and back of neck.

Left hand goes in front of the arm as you hit attacker in face with palm heel.

Side view

*Note, you may also place your right leg behind attackers right leg for tripping action.

Pushing attacker backward and onto the ground.

IDORI

(Kneeling Defence)

Idori is very much a traditional art of Japan. In Wado-Ryu the art of Shinto-Yoshin-Ryu, Master Ohtsukas early training is seen very clearly in the kneeling defence. All Idori needs to be done very fast to get the full impact on the attacker, and you should be careful not to hit the back of your head on the floor when practicing.

HOW TO ATTACK

1. Face your opponent.

2. Za-Rai (seated bow). Bow keeping your eyes on your opponent.

3. Attacker moves forward by placing fists on the floor in front and dragging their body up to their hands twice.

4. At all times keep your eyes on your opponent. Before first move of each attack do 1-4.

(1)

Attacker punches to defenders face with right Junzuki, left knee on the floor, move head slightly to right, hit attacker in face with Teisho (palm heel) off right hand.

Instantly change feet and with left hand knock attacker off their feet, look at 2a. You may also use this but it must be done very fast.

(2)

2a

Using both hands to grab foot.

Attacker grabs defenders collar.
Defender knocks down the attackers
right arm. At same time do a back
hand to stomach.

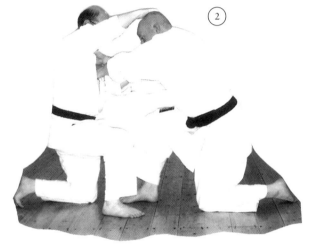

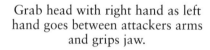
Grab head with right hand as left
hand goes between attackers arms
and grips jaw.

2a

Shows the hand position just prior to
throw.

③

Change feet from right to left
opening up right side for throw.

3a

Side
view
more
open

④

Throw attacker over

⑤

Hit attacker
with right
Uraken to
face.

Attacker punches right Junzuki
on their knee to the face.
Defender gets up and counter
punches with left to face.

Instantly left foot goes behind
attackers right foot, as you hit as
hard as you can with your left hand.
At the same time pull your left foot
back hard, knocking attacker back
onto floor.

At last second, attacker jumps up and tries to punch Junzuki in defenders face with right arm. Move head a little to left and punch up right into stomach, your left hand covers punch.

Come up onto your left leg grabbing the wrist and kicking front kick into stomach. Drag attacker foward onto floor.

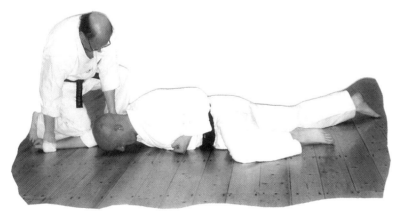

Holding them down with knee and hands.

TACHI-DORI

(Sword Defence)

Whenever I think of Tachi-Dori I think of Master Ohtsuka. I have lost count of the number of times I saw him perform his sword demonstration in Japan and Europe. It was always exciting to watch the great man. Sword defence is of course not for beginners, you need to have a very good understanding of distancing, and you need to be a little brave.

(4) Sword attacker in right stance, defender in right stance a little over a sword length apart.

(2) Attacker steps forward and raises sword above head, defender moves to left, then performs a Teisho to the face or chin of attacker, in between the arms. All movements need to be done very fast.

(3)

Bring your arm back down and immediately punch to ribs. Keep your body out of line of downward sword.

Twist your body and perform a left elbow to the same point as you have just punched.

Attacker swings sword back in an arcing motion from left to right. Defender twists round to left and goes down onto floor, to avoid any chance of sword cutting you on swing.

Sword attacker in left stance, defender in right, attacker
is going to do strike to defenders neck by twisting the
sword sideways as he takes a step forward.

(Note: Sword is
sideways on, it is too
thin to be seen clearly
in the photos)

Twist your back foot (do not move the front foot) and
block the handle of the sword with right open hand.

Move in changing blocking hand from right to left, as you hit attacker in the face with punch.

After a punch do an elbow to body with right arm, bring the right arm back onto the sword handle so for a split second you have two hands on the handle.

To move away, twist to your right as attacker brings sword forward, defender may also do a twisting jump, landing into same stance as photo 5.

Sword attacker in right stance,
defender also in right stance. Attacker
is going to sweep the sword from
right to left.

As sword starts to sweep, defender
leans away from the sword. You now
need to move back in, as sword
reaches its lowest point.

Move back in and perform
back fist (Uraken) to head.

Bring your left foot around and
punch into side of body, your right
hand covering sword arm - see
photo 4a

Like all moves in sword defence,
they must be done fast and with
great care.

⑤ Attacker steps back, defender jumps
around down on to floor avoiding
swinging sword.

The Secret of Karate
is
Looking for the Secret
(Master Hironori Ohtsuka 1892-1982)

Wado-Ryu Kata

The feeling you are trying to get in your mind when performing Kata, is for want of a better word 'total' combat, you must visualise your opponents in your minds eye at all times.

Don't rush your Kata, doing a Kata with power and speed is not the same as rushing the Kata. Try to break down the Kata into sections as you learn them. There is no point in trying to learn a whole Kata in one lesson, as you will almost always forget parts of it.

One of the great things about Kata is as you grow older you can perform the Kata to your fitness level and age. Any Karate-Ka that expects a 60 year old to perform a Kata like a 25 year old is unrealistic. If the 60 year old has been practicing most of their lives then the likelyhood is you would rather watch them perform a faultless Kata, than the 25 year old in the flush of youth.

Kata is very good for fitness and keeps your interest as there is always something new to learn, however you will never learn everything about Kata. This brings me on to variations within different Karate schools, a student that joins a school usually has no idea that he or she might be practicing a Kata or move, different from the founders concept. I was lucky to train with the top instructors from the start. And I have faithfully passed on what I was taught, in this book. However, I am sure some students will be performing some Katas slightly differently. Whatever way you are performing them, I hope I get you thinking about what you are doing and why!

I have performed for the photographs in this book the nine so-called basic Wado-Ryu Katas only once. There is pretty much a general concensus about the similarity of these Katas in most Karate schools. On the other hand there seems to be many different versions of the so-called advanced Katas. I have included two versions of Bassai and Niseishi which I feel merits inclusion in this book. I don't wish to comment on which is best, I will leave that to others, but the feeling I get when performing both the Katas at full speed is the same to me.

Over the years there has been a lot of speculation on the so-called "Lost Kata of Wado-Ryu - Suparinpei". It is clear that Master Ohtsuka did register this Kata at the Budo-Kai in Japan around 1940, he also registered many other things that he never really taught. It is clear to me that Master Ohtsuka did not have much of an interest in this Kata. I have never met anyone that learnt the complete Kata from the Master personally. I want to perform Wado-Ryu Kata that Master Ohtsuka felt was relevant to his art, not something that was introduced for the sake of doing Kata competitions or to look good. It is for this reason I haven't included any information on this Kata in the book.

Master Ohtsuka said that he had given us the Road of Wado-Ryu, but the paths were to be found out by ourselves. This book gives you some of them, but it is only those which we find through our individual efforts that we can really benefit from. On many occasions I would ask Master Ohtsuka "How do you do this movement?" and very often he would reply "Think for yourself". We are all individuals and to perform like clones is not a good idea. As long as there is no major difference in technique, an inch here or a millimetre there makes not a scrap of difference.

PINAN SHODAN

Pinan Shodan is Kata No 1 but nearly always practised second. All the First 5 Pinan Katas are said to have been put together by the famous Karate expert Yasutsune Itosu (1830-1914). They give students a good lead in to the more difficult Katas.

(1) Musubi-Dachi

(2) Yoi
- Move left then right

(3) Double Block
Jodan head
block -
Soto-Uke

(4) Pull left arm in and right arm down.

Step to left in cat stance
Mahanmi-no-nekoashi

(5) Draw left foot back,
Tettsui to face.

(6) Step to right

(7) Repeat 3/4

(8) Draw right foot
back - Tettsui to
face

(9) Turn to your
back. Kick with
right front kick
(Maegeri) at same
time block Jodan-
Soto-Uke. See
photo 18.

(10) Turn back to
the front after
kick. Block
left Shuto-Uke
Jodan

(11) Step block right
Shuto-Uke
Jodan

(12) Step block left
Shuto-Uke
Jodan.

(13)

K

(14)

(15)

(16) Turn to right 90° and perform two more Shuto-Uke Jodan 16/17

Step forward and perform Nukite (Spear hand)

Turn to left 225° and perform two Shuto-Uke

(17)

(18) Move left foot into Gyakuzuki stance, block Soto-Uke Jodan

Reverse view of 18 as you kick.

Kick Maegeri.

(19)

Punch Gyakuzuki

Reverse View of 22

(20) Block left Soto-Uke Jodan

Reverse view of 20

(21)

Kick Maegeri left leg step down.

(22)

Punch Gyakuzuki

K ㉓

㉓a

Step forward into
Junzuki stance.
Block Soto-Uke
Jodan.

㉓b

Reverse view

㉔

Turn left 225°, block
Gedan-Barai left.

㉕

Step same angle
block Jodan-Uke
right.

㉖

Turn 90° into
right Junzuki
stance, block
Gedan-Barai.

㉗

Step same
angle, block
left Jodan-Uke

㉘

Draw back
left foot

㉙

Back to
Musubi-Dachi

3

4

Application
example
3/4

110

PINAN NIDAN

Pinan Nidan, Kata No 2. When doing the first five Pinan Katas a good tip for 1, 2, 4, & 5 is you should finish where your start point was. If you do, your stances will be the right length.

1

Musubi-Dachi

2

Yoi

Step out with left foot into Mahanmi-no-Nekoashi, blocking down with left Tettsui.

3

4

5

Step and punch right Junzuki

6

Turn 180° block to right Gedan-Barai

7

Draw your right foot back and block down Tettsui.

8

9

Step and punch left Junzuki

Application 3/4

Turn 90° to left.

Block Gedan-Barai.

12/13/14
Do 3 steps
performing
Jodan-Uke
(head blocks)
3 times.

K

Turn 225° and block Gedan-Barai.

Step and punch Junzuki

Application 7/8

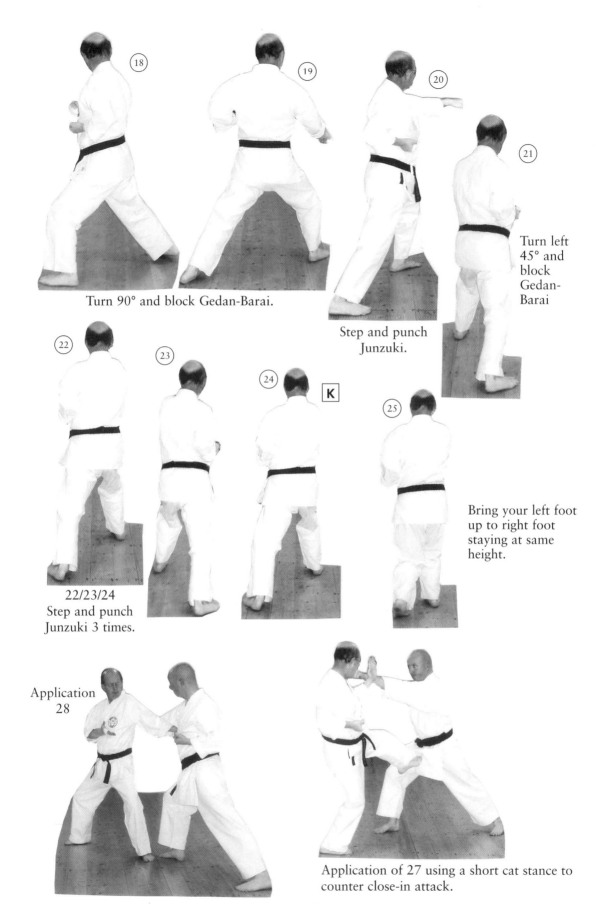

Turn 90° and block Gedan-Barai.

Turn left 45° and block Gedan-Barai

Step and punch Junzuki.

K

Bring your left foot up to right foot staying at same height.

22/23/24
Step and punch Junzuki 3 times.

Application 28

Application of 27 using a short cat stance to counter close-in attack.

114

Turn to left 225° into Neko-ashi (cat stance) keeping body same height

(26)

(27) Left hand on top

(28) Step with left and perform Nukite (spear hand), stance is Shiko-Dachi.

(29) Step forward with right and strike Nukite with right hand

Keep your body same height turn 90° to right.

(30)

(31) Right hand on top

(32) Step with right and strike Nukite with right hand.

(33) Step and strike Nukite with left hand both 33/34 you are in Shiko-Dachi stance

(34) Bring foot back to Yama.

(25) Then back to Musubi-Dachi

PINAN SANDAN

Pinan Sandan Kata 3 gives students a good grounding in Shiko-Dachi stance (see photo above), as well as good practice for using your hands in double blocks using each hand differently.

(1) Musubi-Dachi

(2) Yoi

(3) Left Soto-Uke Jodan (Face) your stance is Mashomen-No-Neko-Ashi (Cat Stance). Turn to left 90° blocking.

(4) Step up with right foot.

Block Soto-Uke right arm and Gedan-Bari left arm at same time.

(5)

(6) Block again Soto-Uke (left arm) and Gedan-Barai (right arm).

(7) Go back with your right leg and turn 180° into Neko-Ashi.

(8)

(9) Step up with left foot.

As soon as you turn block Jodan Soto-Uke

Block Jodan Soto-Uke with left arm and Gedan-Barai with right.

Block Jodan Soto-Uke with right then Gedan-Barai with left.

Step out with left foot, turn 90° to front and block Soto-Uke Jodan again.

K

Step and do Nukite to body with right hand.

K

Application of 14/15/16

14a

Step across with back foot 180° bringing right hand onto lower back.

Turning 180° and do Tettsui with left arm, then step Junzuki punch with right.

15a

16b

Turn left by bringing your left to right, your feet are now in Musubi-Dachi.

Step forward and block with your right elbow, followed by side hammer fist to body (Tettsui). Draw arm back to body. This is repeated in step 20. On 21 The Tettsui is left out as you step into 22, left Junzuki punch.

K

18a

19a

19b

19c

Side views of
18 & 19

Applications for 19a-19b

(23) Bring your right foot up, turn 180° and do a backward elbow (Empi) with left and punch over left shoulder.

(24)

(25)

(26) Step to your right.

(27)

(28)

(29)

Do right elbow to body and punch over right shoulder. Move right foot back into Yama stance.

Yama

Musubi-Dachi

PINAN YONDAN

Pinan Yondan, Kata 4. This Kata uses for the first time in a Kata, a sweeping block called Hari-Uke (see photo above). This move is used three times in Ku-Shanku Kata. It is said that Yasutsune Itosu made Pinan Yondan mainly from Ku-Shanku.

Step to left into Neko-ashi stance, block with left arm

Bring your left foot back to original position, step out and block to right.

Musubi-dachi

Yoi

Bring your right foot towards left

Step into left Junzuki stance crossing your arms to make a block.

Step again into Neko-ashi stance block Soto-Uke Jodan

Side view

Bring your left foot up to your right

Kick Maegeri and left Gedan-Barai at the same time

Twist your body into Gyakuzuki stance and do an Empi.

Bring right foot to left

Kick Maegeri to right and right Gedan-Barai.

Left Empi on both 10/13, your other hand goes on to front of Empi arm.

Turn your body to left, sweep your right arm across body.

Kick Maegeri

After kick, step down and bring your left knee into the back of right knee.

K

Punch downward with Uraken onto bridge of nose, as you bring up your back leg.

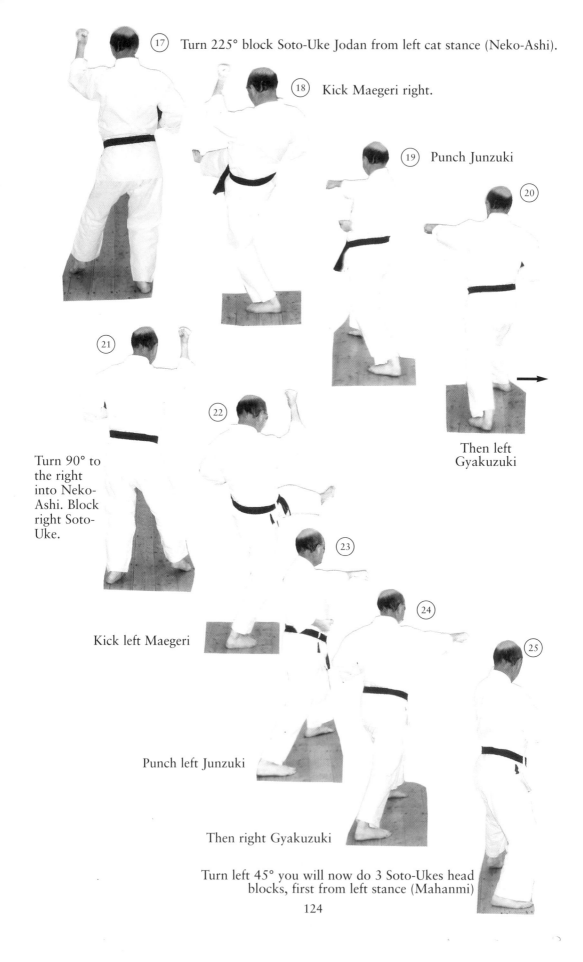

(17) Turn 225° block Soto-Uke Jodan from left cat stance (Neko-Ashi).

(18) Kick Maegeri right.

(19) Punch Junzuki

(20)

Then left
Gyakuzuki

(21)

Turn 90° to
the right
into Neko-
Ashi. Block
right Soto-
Uke.

(22)

Kick left Maegeri

(23)

(24)

(25)

Punch left Junzuki

Then right Gyakuzuki

Turn left 45° you will now do 3 Soto-Ukes head
blocks, first from left stance (Mahanmi)

124

(26)

(27)

Now right stance then left stance once more. Each move your stance will be Neko-Ashi your non-blocking arm is on your chest.

(28)

Twist your body to left squaring it up into short cat stance as you block with right and left Soto-Uke.

(29)

K

Pull your both arms down as you bring knee up.

(30)

Turn 225°

(31)

Block Kake-Uke with left.

(32)

Turn 90° putting your heel down first

(33)

In 31/33 non Kake-Uke hand blocks down with Teisho.

(34)

(35)

Block Kake-Uke with right arm. Right foot back to Yama.

Yama

Musubi-Dachi

Side view of No 15

Application of 14

Block grab
and punch

Knocking hand down with left hand
then punch.

31a

Application

31b

PINAN GODAN

Pinan Godan, Kata 5. For the first time a jump is used within the Kata. You need strong legs to get the best out of Pinan Godan, you change direction using quick light movements, which come into play more in the Kata Chinto. The hand movement in the middle of the Kata is a little difficult, therefore you should study the photos' carefully.

Musubi-Dachi

Yoi

Turn to the left into cat stance (Mashomen) Soto-Uke Jodan.

Punch on spot

Bring your right foot to left.

Turn 90° to right, block Soto-Uke Jodan

Punch on spot

Bring your left foot to your right.

Application 3/4

(9) Step forward with right and block Soto-Uke Jodan your stance being Neko-Ashi (Mahanmi).

(10) Take one step forward and block.

(11) Bring both arms upward then keeping hands together roll your hands down to stop point. Study photo 12 carefully.

(12)

(13) Block out with right arm.

Punch Junzuki with right arm.

K (14)

Turn left 180° into Shiko-Dachi, block Gedan-Barai with right arm.

(15)

(16) Draw your left foot back and block with left arm.

129

Take step forward into Junzuki stance and perform Empi.

Bring your left foot up, block Soto-Uke

Jump into air getting your heels, feet and knees up.

Move your left foot backwards, punch out to face, leaning backwards.

On landing keep your back straight and do a X block.

K

Take a step and block same as Pinan Shodan photo 23.

Draw back your left foot.

Step out with your right foot as you block.

Twist and lean away as you do two blocks, as in photo 25.

Move your left foot back first into Yama.

26 27

Yama

Musubi-Dachi

Application for 19

11a

Application for 11-14

12b

13c

14d

131

KUSHANKU

Kushanku Kata is said to have been based on the teachings of a Chinese official named Koshokun (1760-?) who is said to have come to Okinawa. No one seems to know whether 1760 is the date he was born or the date he came to Okinawa. Don't attempt to learn this Kata until you have a good grounding in the 5 Pinan Katas.

(1)

Musubi-Dachi

*Note: Kushanku Yoi is a little wider than normal yoi.

Start bringing your arms up and make a circle around and down to no 4.

(2)

Yoi

(3)

(4)

(5) Step to left into Neko-Ashi.

Block to right by bringing your left leg towards your right around half way.

(6)

(7) Move your right foot back, left hand ready to block.

Block (8) and then punch with right hand (9).

Step to left your feet being the same as Gyakuzuki-no-Tsukkomi but body a little higher. Block right Soto-Uke.

Bring your left foot up into Yoi stance and punch with left.

Step with right doing same as photo 10 but with left Soto-Uke.

Bring your left foot up to right, turn and kick backwards the same as photo 9 Pinan Shodan.

14-17 all the same as Pinan Shodan

K

(17)

(18)

Side view of 19

Kick Maegeri with
right, see photo 23.

Turn 180° left
and do the same
movement as
Pinan Yodan
photo 14 and
22/23 of this
page.

After kick turn your body to
left going down, block Gedan-
Barai, right hand covering your
head like Jodan-Uke block.

(19)

Bring left arm
back, as you
move right hand
forward.

(20)

(21)

(22)

Turn left,
same
movement
as 18

Kick Maegeri

(23)

As your kick
lands on the
floor turn into
same as 19
photo. This
movement is
the same for
18.

Stand up block
with left hand or
back hand
punch. See 21a
in applications.

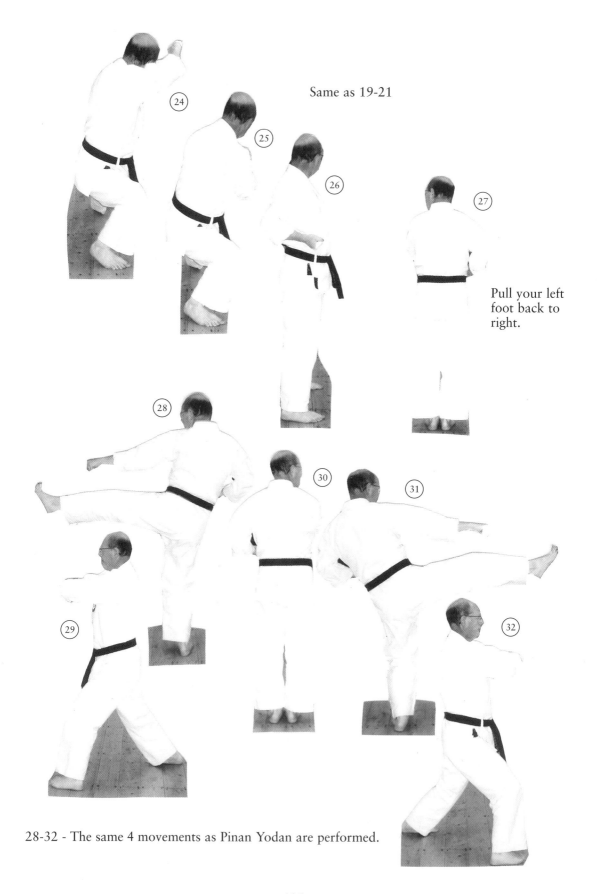

Same as 19-21

Pull your left foot back to right.

28-32 - The same 4 movements as Pinan Yodan are performed.

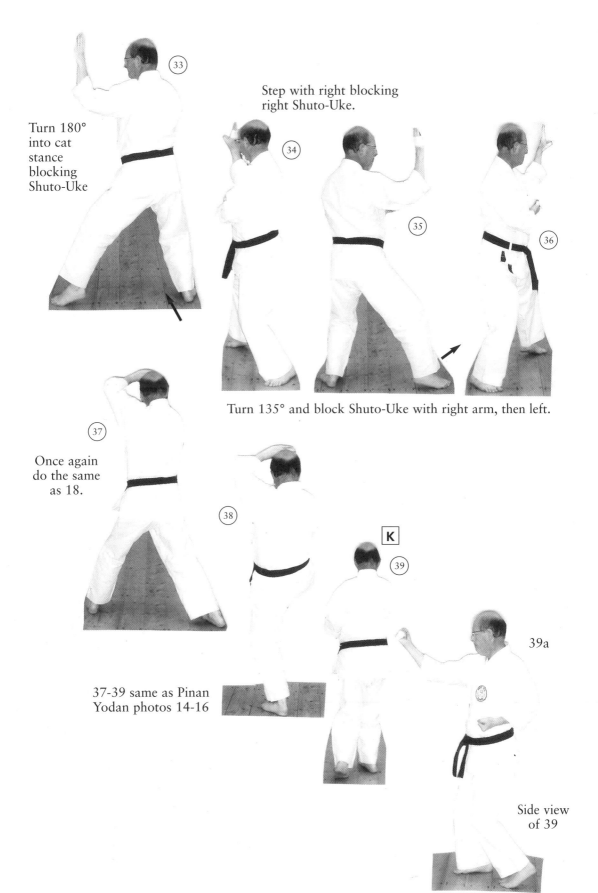

Turn 180° into cat stance blocking Shuto-Uke

(33)

Step with right blocking right Shuto-Uke.

(34)

(35)

(36)

Turn 135° and block Shuto-Uke with right arm, then left.

Once again do the same as 18.

(37)

(38)

K

(39)

39a

37-39 same as Pinan Yodan photos 14-16

Side view of 39

137

Move back and block
Soto-Uke Jodan.

 41-42 - Punch like Gyakuzuki
then Junzuki.

Turn back
to left 180°,
open left
hand, close
right.

Bring knee up as
you bring fist
and hand
together.

 Drop your body down
with hand resting on
the floor with
shoulders wide apart.

 Turn your body 180°. As you
come up block Shuto-Uke left
then step right, both stances are
in Neko-Ashi (Mahanmi).

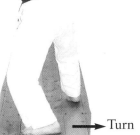 Turn

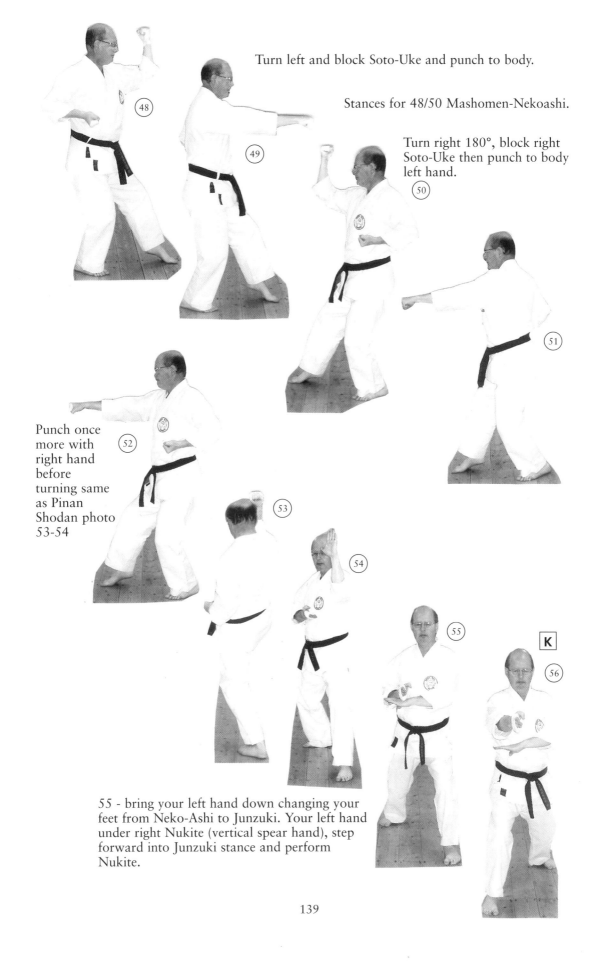

Turn left and block Soto-Uke and punch to body.

Stances for 48/50 Mashomen-Nekoashi.

Turn right 180°, block right Soto-Uke then punch to body left hand.

Punch once more with right hand before turning same as Pinan Shodan photo 53-54

55 - bring your left hand down changing your feet from Neko-Ashi to Junzuki. Your left hand under right Nukite (vertical spear hand), step forward into Junzuki stance and perform Nukite.

K

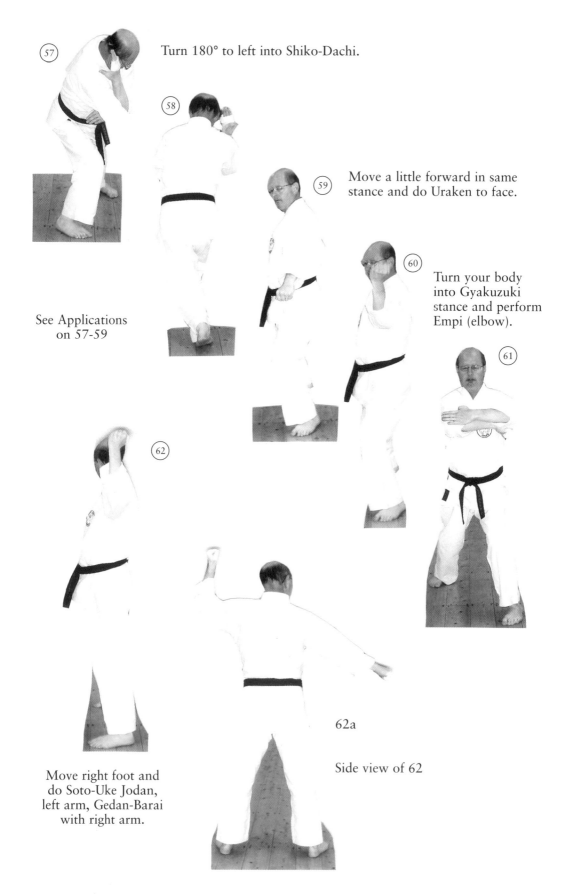

57 Turn 180° to left into Shiko-Dachi.

58

59 Move a little forward in same stance and do Uraken to face.

60 Turn your body into Gyakuzuki stance and perform Empi (elbow).

61

See Applications on 57-59

62

62a

Side view of 62

Move right foot and do Soto-Uke Jodan, left arm, Gedan-Barai with right arm.

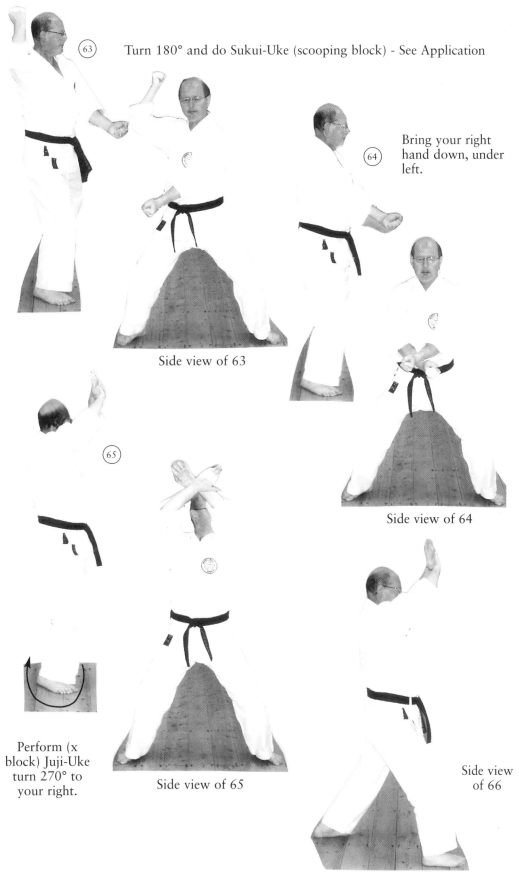

(63) Turn 180° and do Sukui-Uke (scooping block) - See Application

Side view of 63

(64) Bring your right hand down, under left.

Side view of 64

(65)

Side view of 65

Perform (x block) Juji-Uke turn 270° to your right.

Side view of 66

K

Bring your hands down into fist, then jump into the air, kick with right foot, landing in Junzuki stance. At the point of landing do Uraken Jodan.

Side view of 67

Turn 270° keeping back upright to right.

Left hand under right.

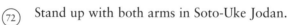

Stand up with both arms in Soto-Uke Jodan.

Draw back your right foot into same as start.

Left foot then right back into Musubi-Dachi.

142

APPLICATIONS

54a

56a

57-58

59a

21a

63a

63b

70a

70b

70c

19

144

NAIHANCHI

Naihanchi Kata; was, it is said Master Ohtsukas favoured Kata. It is certainly a difficult one and demands intensive training. The main points of the Kata should be moving into Naihanchi stance, after punching and blocking, pulling back into the same arm level (approximately level with mid-sternum) and relaxing during the Kata especially the shoulders, that need to be kept in a normal state. This Kata is great for strengthening your legs and calf muscles, it is said Ohtsukas main influence for this Kata was the Karate Master Motobu.

Place left hand on top of right, make a circle, in a calm way.

End with right hand just touching left.

Musubi-Dachi

Heisoku-Dachi
stance

Drop your body, lift up arms and step with left to the right, then right foot into Naihanchi stance.

Bring hands up and turn them over trying to keep your elbows from coming out. From photo 6 look left then right as if looking across a battlefield.

Block with right side of hand Shuto (knife block).

Your stance now for rest of the Kata will be <u>Naihanchi stance,</u> feet a little inwards.

Twist body to the right and do Empi.

Twist body back to prepare for next movement, left arm block down Gedan-Barai

11-15 you are looking left

Punch out at 45° to left.

*It is important you do not move the Gedan-Barai block until you pull back punch. It should be done at the same time.

Step with right then left into Naihanchi stance.

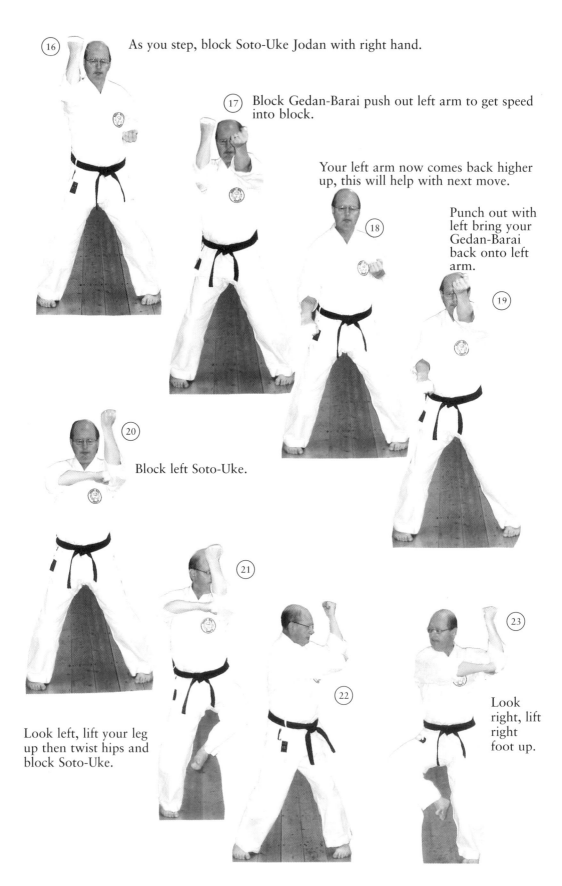

As you step, block Soto-Uke Jodan with right hand.

Block Gedan-Barai push out left arm to get speed into block.

Your left arm now comes back higher up, this will help with next move.

Punch out with left bring your Gedan-Barai back onto left arm.

Block left Soto-Uke.

Look left, lift your leg up then twist hips and block Soto-Uke.

Look right, lift right foot up.

Block Soto-
Uke to
right.

(24)

Look left placing left arm ready to do double
punch.

(25)

(26) **K**

Be careful you
do not over
punch with
right arm.

(27) Draw back left arm.

(28) Right Empi to body.

(29)

Twist to
right, look
right, right
arm ready to
block.

Try at all times to keep Naihanchi stance.

150

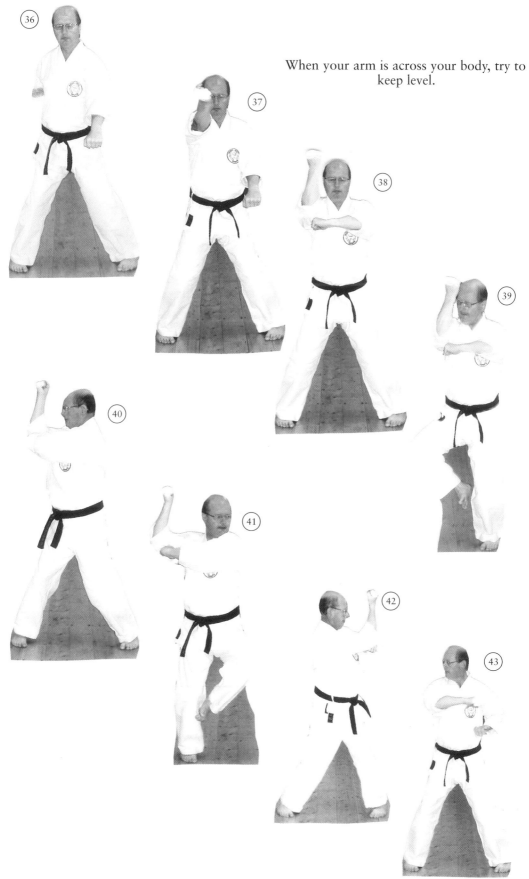

When your arm is across your body, try to keep level.

K ㊹ Bring your right foot back into Heisoku-Dachi..

㊺

㊻

17a

Musubi-Dachi

20a

27a

Applications

152

SEISHAN

Seishan Kata - The first half is performed with tension. By using tension in this way, we learn how to control our bodies. Control over your body is control over your Art. When performing the tension should be a nice flowing action, not a jagged movement. The history seems to say that this Kata was introduced into Okinawa by Bushi Matsumura, but the dates are obscure.

Go into Seishan stance using tension block Soto-Uke left Chudan (body).

Musub-Dachi

Yoi

Punch down at around the height of your belt.

Step forward in a semi-circular movement dropping your arm just a little below your arm on your hip.

Block Soto-Uke right Chudan

154

Step once more drop your arm as you step and block Soto-Uke with left arm once more.

Punch down again.

See Applications for 12-16

Bring your right hand back together, go up so as you block with your elbows then coming down again go out to the front of your body. Your hands during these moves are in Haito.

Open hand and bring back as shown in photo.

(16) Bring down hands, you are performing knife hand blocks.

(17)

Step with right foot, turn into Seishan stance 180°.

Block Gedan-Barai with left hand Soto-Uke with right hand. Pull back right hand.

18 is the reverse of 19 a,b and c.

(18)

You are now going to do three movements on each step forward.

19a

Back view of 19 is just reverse of 18.

Cross hands block Gedan-Barai and Soto-Uke block.

19b

19c

19c - pull back left hand. This move is called Kake-Uke (hooking on grabbing movement).

Step forward into right.

(19)

20a

Before 20a do 19a but left hand on top.

20b

Repeat 18

(20)

(21) K

Twist right 90° into Tata-Seishan.

(22)

Punch left and right.

(23)

From move 21 all movements are done at normal speed.

*All movement from 1-20 are done under tension in a nice flowing action.

Turn 180° block Jodan Soto-Uke left arm punch right/left.

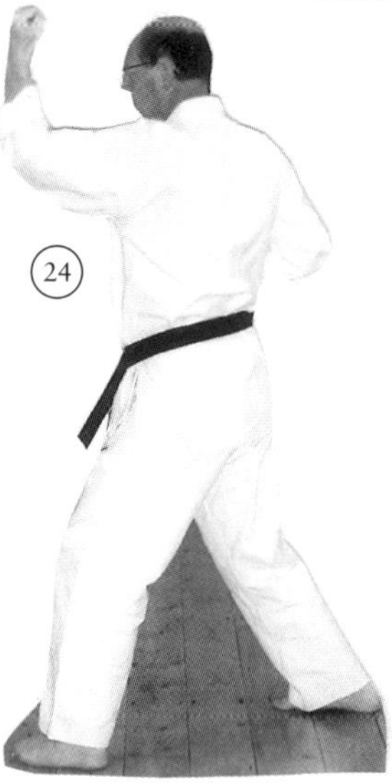

Turn 90° punch left/right.

Bring your knee up,
and at the same time
perform back fist to
face, twist 180°.

*From 21-29 all stances are Tata-Seishan.

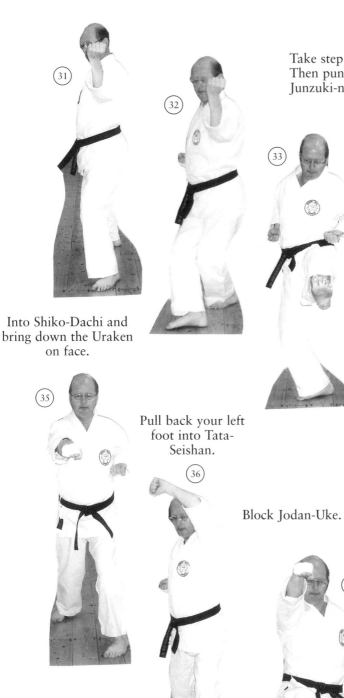

Take step with right foot, kick Maegeri.
Then punch to groin, same stance as
Junzuki-no-Tsukkomi.

Into Shiko-Dachi and
bring down the Uraken
on face.

Pull back your left
foot into Tata-
Seishan.

Block Jodan-Uke.

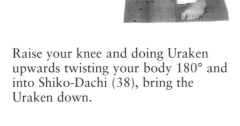

Raise your knee and doing Uraken
upwards twisting your body 180° and
into Shiko-Dachi (38), bring the
Uraken down.

(39)

(40)

Repeat 31-38 from other side.

(41)

(42)

(43)

(44)

(45)

(46)

(47) K

44-45 same as 30-31

Step back into Tate-Seishan.

Do Mikazuki-Geri (Crescent Kick) towards your left hand.

(48) Draw back left foot to do palm hand block.

(49) Move left foot back to Yama.

(50) Musubi-Dachi

48a

15a

16a

APPLICATIONS

33a

34a

12a

13a

43/44

46a

CHINTO

Chinto Kata is possibly Chinese. The story goes that Bushi Matsumura learnt it from a Chinese sailor. It's main difficulty is balancing during the turns and standing on one leg, this is why it comes into the advanced Katas of Wado-Ryu.

① Musub-Dachi

② Yoi

There has been a lot of talk over the years on the start to Chinto. If the first move should be Tate-Seishan or Kokutsu-Dachi (modified for Chinto) in application. I have included Tata-Seishan. My own view is the old way seems to get more power into the start of the Kata.

③ Step back, stance both feet flat on the floor, bring both hands up keeping your elbow down.

④ Bring arms down the same as Pinan Godan, your arm a little more to your left side.

⑤ Block out

⑥ **K** Twist your body as you punch into Tate-Seishan.

⑦ Block Gedan-Barai stance Shiko-Dachi.

Twist 360° to your left blocking with your right arm as you twist round, and as you get ready for blocking.

⑧

164

Turn 90° bring up both arms in x block.

Pull arms down and jump Nidan-Geri kicking with left leg.

K

Block as you land x block.

Turn 180° to right block same as 11.

Turn back 180° using same feet movement as Pinan Godan for stances 13/14

Block Gedan-Barai with right hand, left hand on chest. Step into left block the same but hand open, one more step placing right hand in front of left and open them palm front.

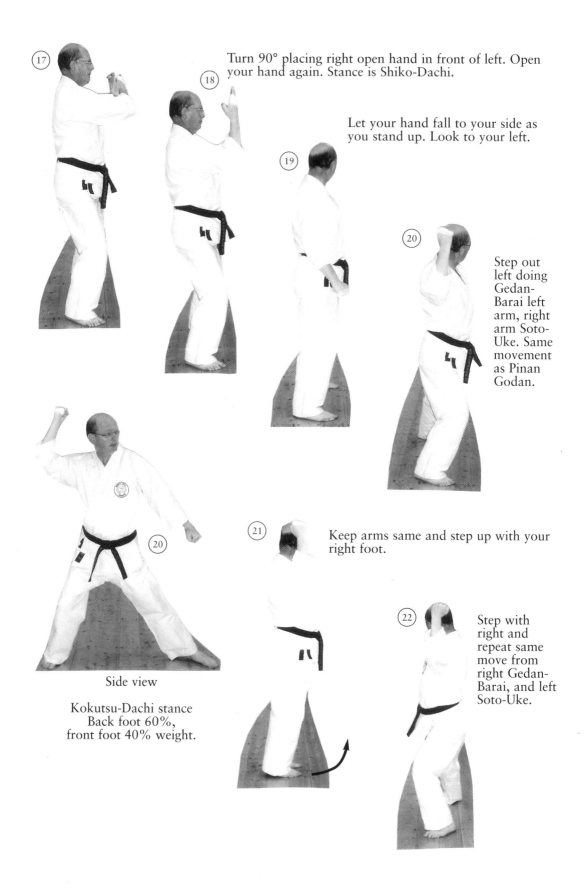

(17)

(18) Turn 90° placing right open hand in front of left. Open your hand again. Stance is Shiko-Dachi.

Let your hand fall to your side as you stand up. Look to your left.

(19)

(20) Step out left doing Gedan-Barai left arm, right arm Soto-Uke. Same movement as Pinan Godan.

(20)

Side view

Kokutsu-Dachi stance
Back foot 60%,
front foot 40% weight.

(21) Keep arms same and step up with your right foot.

(22) Step with right and repeat same move from right Gedan-Barai, and left Soto-Uke.

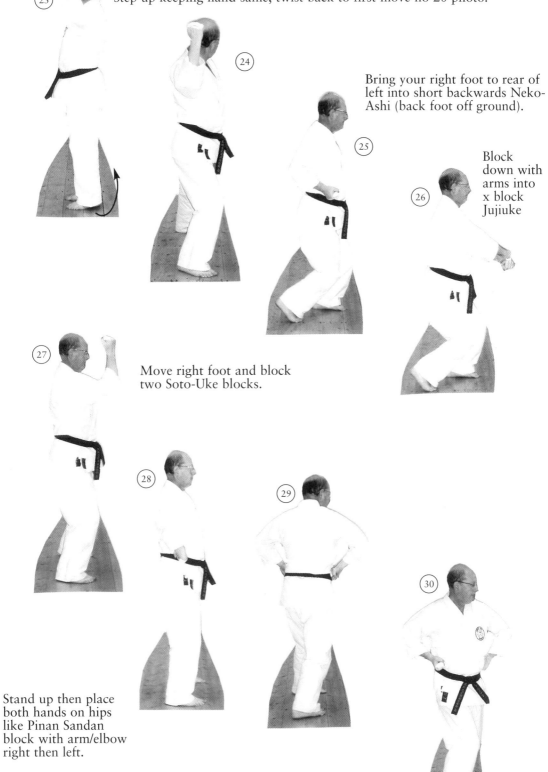

23 Step up keeping hand same, twist back to first move no 20 photo.

24

25 Bring your right foot to rear of left into short backwards Neko-Ashi (back foot off ground).

26 Block down with arms into x block Jujiuke

27 Move right foot and block two Soto-Uke blocks.

28

29

30

Stand up then place both hands on hips like Pinan Sandan block with arm/elbow right then left.

Turn 180° blocking Soto-Uke with both hands.

(31)

Block to your left placing your foot on calf, at same time block Gedan-Barai, and Soto-Uke Jodan.

(32)

Bring your hand back the same as Pinan Yodan.

(33)

(34)

Block and kick same time.

K (35)

Step and punch Junzuki.

(36)

(37)

Bring hand back like Pinan Yodan.

Draw back your right foot and repeat same as 32. This time block Gedan-Barai right Soto-Uke left.

(38) Kick and block Gedan-Barai.

*Note all
3 kicks are
Maegeri.

(39) Punch Gyakuzuki in Tate-Seishan stance.

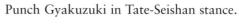

Turn 180° and perform
same movements as 32-34.

(42)

(43)

Punch right Gyakuzuki in
Tata-Seishan

(44)

(45)

Twist
into
Empi,
Tata
Seishan
stance.

Turn 180° into Shiko-Dachi stance and
block Kake-Uke.

Bring your arms down getting ready to throw your back fist Uraken to face, your left arm on to right arm. Turn to right 180° and try to keep your balance as your left leg goes on your calf.

Block out Gedan-Barai as you kick Maegeri with left leg.

K Step and punch Junzuki.

Turn 180° back to Yama.

Yama

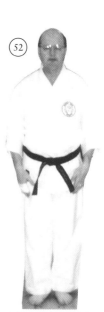

Musubi-Dachi

170

TATE-SEISHAN (CHINTO)

Photo 3

44a/45a

APPLICATIONS

47a

13a

26a

42a

BASSAI

I have included two versions of Bassai, both have their own merit. It is a difficult Kata to perform well. There are many versons of this Kata including those practiced by other styles. These include Matsumura Bassai and Tomari-no-Bassai. The Kata finishes by three blocks representing looking for someone in the dark.

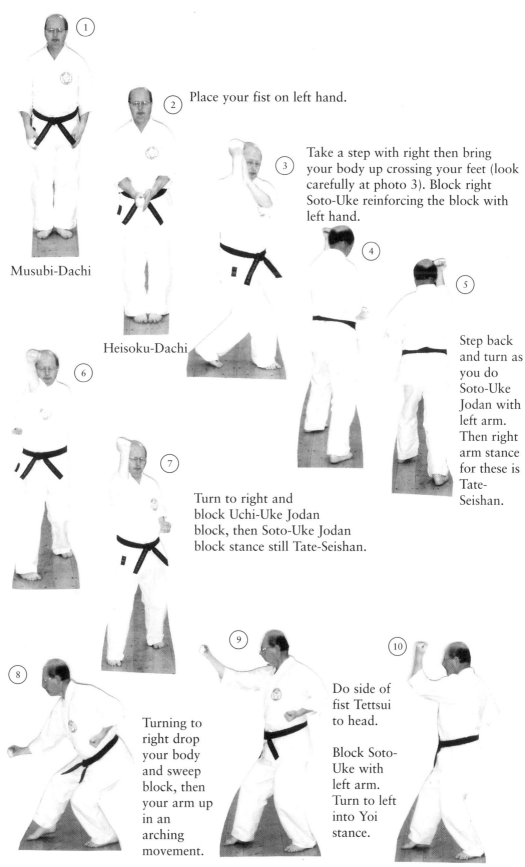

1

Musubi-Dachi

2 Place your fist on left hand.

3 Take a step with right then bring your body up crossing your feet (look carefully at photo 3). Block right Soto-Uke reinforcing the block with left hand.

Heisoku-Dachi

4

5 Step back and turn as you do Soto-Uke Jodan with left arm. Then right arm stance for these is Tate-Seishan.

6

7 Turn to right and block Uchi-Uke Jodan block, then Soto-Uke Jodan block stance still Tate-Seishan.

8 Turning to right drop your body and sweep block, then your arm up in an arching movement.

9 Do side of fist Tettsui to head.

10 Block Soto-Uke with left arm. Turn to left into Yoi stance.

(11) Bring left arm in front of body.

(12) Block out.

(13) Then punch again right arm.

(14) Step out to left and do same movement as Ku-Shanku Kata 12-16.

(15)

(16) Do same movement as Ku-Shanku.

(17)

(18)

(19)

After last left Jodan Soto-Uke block bring left foot up to right. Step forward with right into right Shuto-Uke head block stance as always with this block Neko-Ashi.

Step into left block once more Shuto-Uke.

Then back into right one more Shuto-Uke.

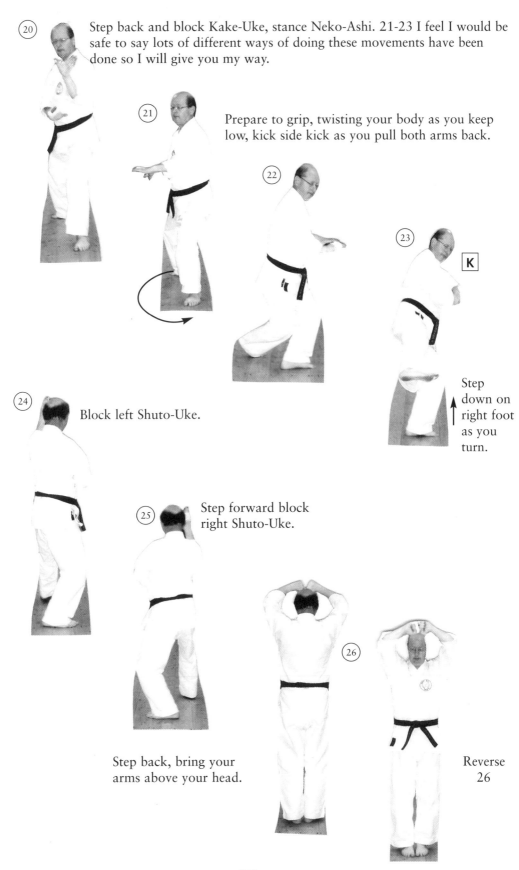

(20) Step back and block Kake-Uke, stance Neko-Ashi. 21-23 I feel I would be safe to say lots of different ways of doing these movements have been done so I will give you my way.

(21) Prepare to grip, twisting your body as you keep low, kick side kick as you pull both arms back.

(22)

(23)

K

Step down on right foot as you turn.

(24) Block left Shuto-Uke.

(25) Step forward block right Shuto-Uke.

Step back, bring your arms above your head.

(26)

Reverse 26

175

(27)

Step back in and do two Tettsui to side of body then move slightly forward and punch front hand Junzuki.

Reverse of 27

Bring your left foot up to your right, block Soto-Uke Jodan and Chudan-Uke body block.

(28)

Side view of 28

(29)

Side view of 29

Step forward into Shiko-Dachi and block Gedan-Barai.

(30)

Bring your left foot up to right into Yoi stance.

Side view of 30

31. Swing your right leg around, touch hand bringing foot down into Shiko-Dachi stance.

32. Strike your elbow against left hand.

33. Block/strike Tettsui to body.

34. Bring arm back to give momentum to movement and do it once more.

35.

Side view of 33-35.

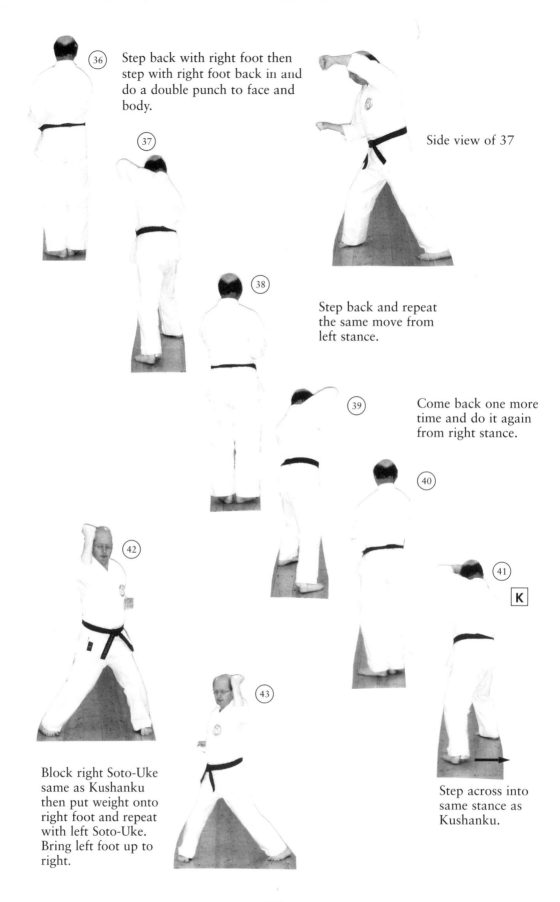

(36) Step back with right foot then step with right foot back in and do a double punch to face and body.

(37)

Side view of 37

(38) Step back and repeat the same move from left stance.

(39) Come back one more time and do it again from right stance.

(40)

(42)

(41)

K

(43)

Block right Soto-Uke same as Kushanku then put weight onto right foot and repeat with left Soto-Uke. Bring left foot up to right.

Step across into same stance as Kushanku.

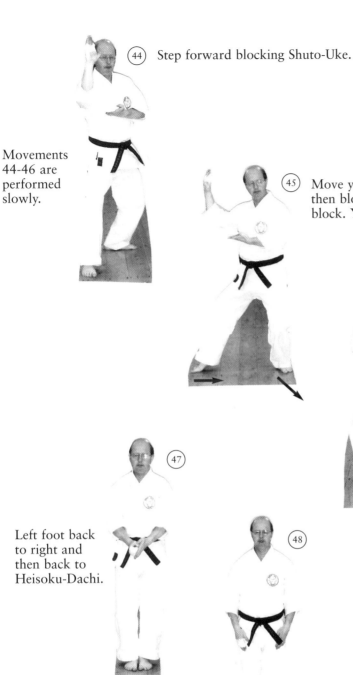

(44) Step forward blocking Shuto-Uke.

Movements 44-46 are performed slowly.

(45) Move your right foot fast to right, then block slowly as you do this block. You are still looking left.

(46)

Bring your right foot up to your left fast, then block slowly.

(47)

Left foot back to right and then back to Heisoku-Dachi.

(48)

Musubi-Dachi

BASSAI 2

There are a number of moves that change the kata. Most of the kata is the same as Bassai I. The feeling of the kata as you do it comes across the same.

Musubi-Dachi

Don't cross leg at this point but keep leg forward as in photo.

Heisoku-Dachi

Same as
Bassai 1

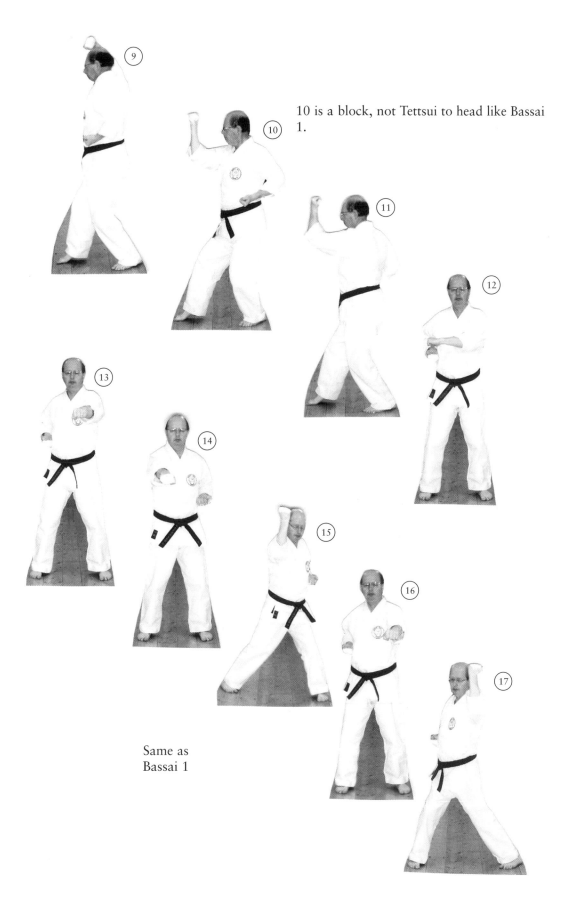

10 is a block, not Tettsui to head like Bassai 1.

Same as
Bassai 1

181

Movement 22 dropping your body very low come up with right hand at sharp angle. Just let your left hand go with the twist of your body to end up like photo 22.

K

Same as Bassai 1

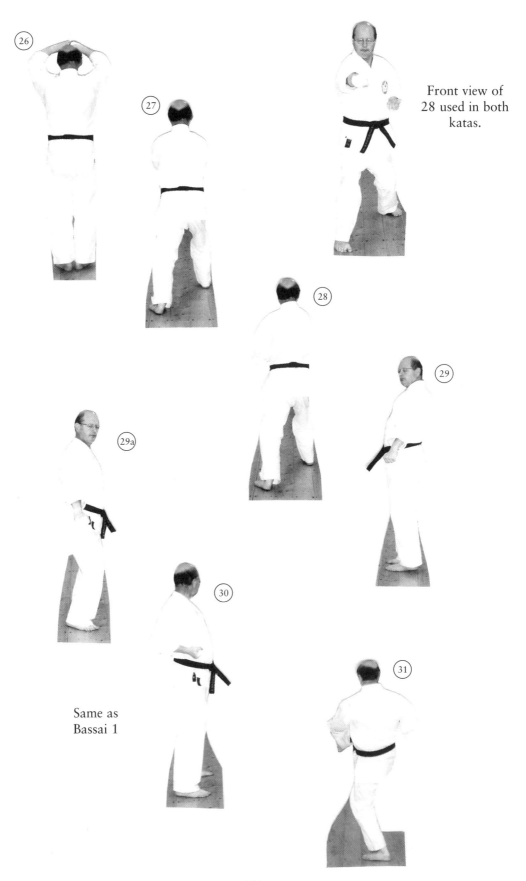

Front view of 28 used in both katas.

Same as Bassai 1

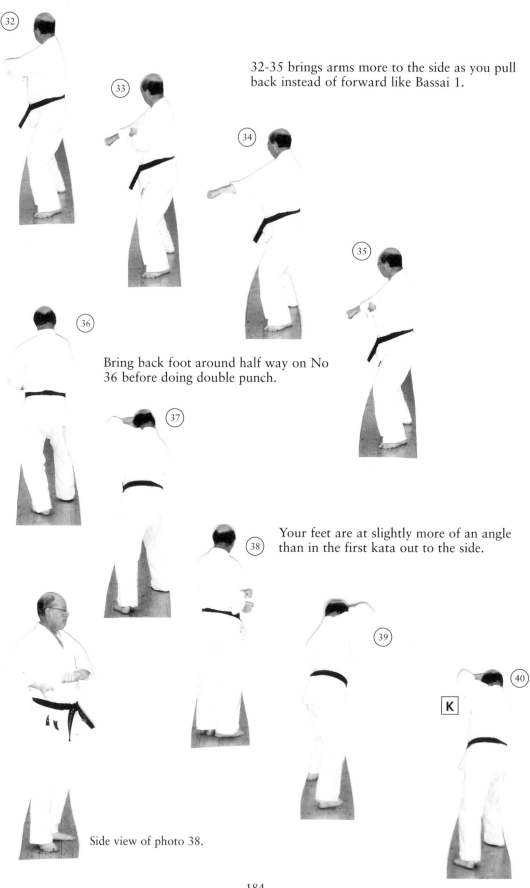

32-35 brings arms more to the side as you pull back instead of forward like Bassai 1.

Bring back foot around half way on No 36 before doing double punch.

Your feet are at slightly more of an angle than in the first kata out to the side.

K

Side view of photo 38.

Heisoku-Dachi

Musubi-Dachi

185

26a

27a

22a

31a

ROHAI

This Kata seems to originally come from Master Itosu. It is a nice Kata to do, not too long. It should be learned before Wanshu Kata as the movement where you turn around and block Shuto-Uke is the same movement on the ground as Wanshu is in the air.

① Musubi-Dachi

② Heisoku-Dachi

③ Step out to right into Naihanchi stance.

Crossing your arms, tense your arms a little pulling back strongly.

④

⑤ Bring arms up, back of hands together.

⑥ Open hands.

⑦ Look left, bring left arm up to head, right hand open.

188

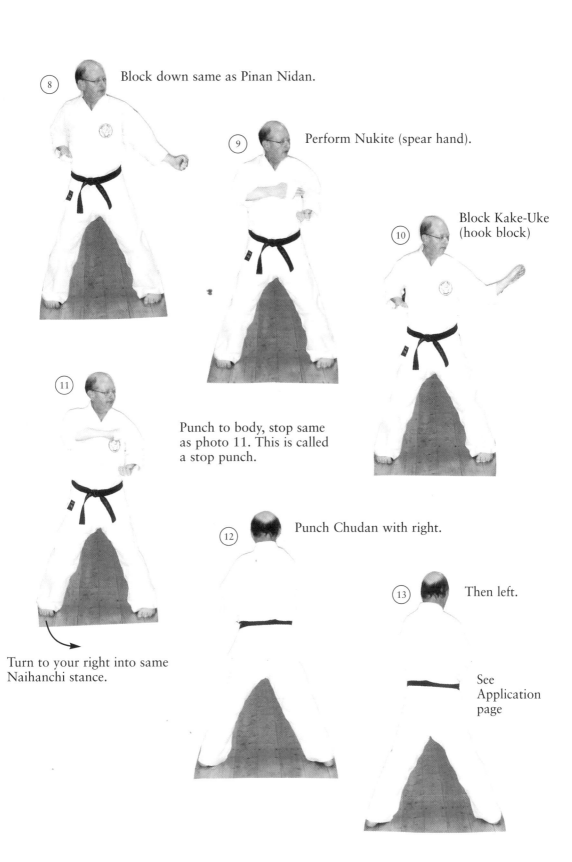

Block down same as Pinan Nidan.

Perform Nukite (spear hand).

Block Kake-Uke (hook block)

Punch to body, stop same as photo 11. This is called a stop punch.

Turn to your right into same Naihanchi stance.

Punch Chudan with right.

Then left.

See Application page

(14)

Bring right foot
up with hand
turned to your
right

(14a)

Rear view

(15)

Block same as
Pinan Nidan, but
front foot is flat
on floor.

(16)

(17)

Repeat 14

(18)

Repeat 15

(19) Step punch right Junzuki.

(20) Move right foot back around half way, bring right arm to body, see photo 22.

(21) Step with right foot into Tate-Seishan performing a double punch.

(22) Step back with right foot get ready for next move.

(23) Step with left double punch.

(24) Step back with left.

(25) Step into right one more time performing a double punch again.

K

Step around with your feet until you are in left stance and block Shuto-Uke same as Pinan Shodan.

Step into left and perform one more Shuto-Uke.

Move right foot and cross hands back into Naihanchi stance.

Move left a little then right back to Heisoku-Dachi.

Musubi-Dachi

12a

Rear view of 12/13

12a

12a

13a

21a

14a

APPLICATIONS

15a

193

JION

Jion seems to have lost some of its history, but may be the name of a Buddhist monk.
It is a strong Kata with lots of powerful moves.

Step back into right Junzuki stance, block right Soto-Uke and left Gedan-Barai.

Heisoku-Dachi

Step with left into Neko-Ashi crossing right hand over left.

Do not pull right hand back just punch as your foot touches the floor from right Maegeri into Junzuki stance.

8/9

Move your right foot to your right and into cat stance Neko-Ashi crossing arms right in front of left hand.

Gyakuzuki and Junzuki once more.

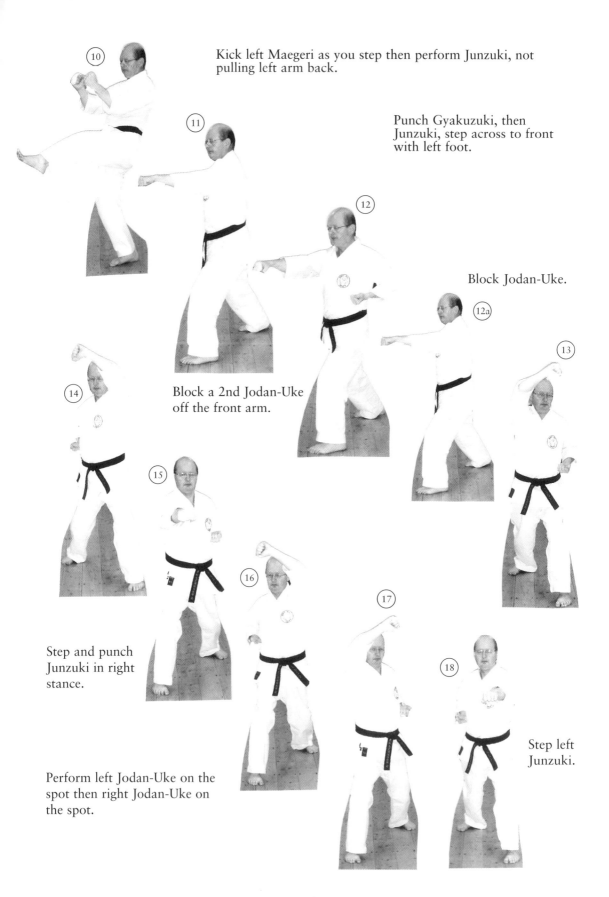

Kick left Maegeri as you step then perform Junzuki, not pulling left arm back.

Punch Gyakuzuki, then Junzuki, step across to front with left foot.

Block Jodan-Uke.

Block a 2nd Jodan-Uke off the front arm.

Step and punch Junzuki in right stance.

Perform left Jodan-Uke on the spot then right Jodan-Uke on the spot.

Step left Junzuki.

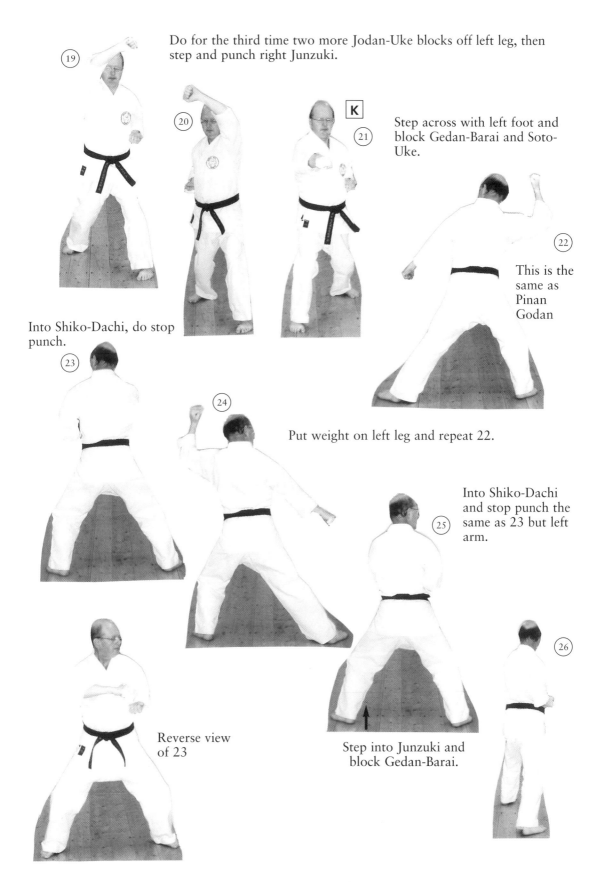

(19)

Do for the third time two more Jodan-Uke blocks off left leg, then step and punch right Junzuki.

(20)

(21) **K**

Step across with left foot and block Gedan-Barai and Soto-Uke.

(22)

This is the same as Pinan Godan

Into Shiko-Dachi, do stop punch.

(23)

(24)

Put weight on left leg and repeat 22.

(25)

Into Shiko-Dachi and stop punch the same as 23 but left arm.

Reverse view of 23

(26)

Step into Junzuki and block Gedan-Barai.

Stop and perform Teisho to face three times.

Side view of 27

Again perform double block.

Step to right, right foot to left and bring feet together. Perform back fist with left arm, right arm on chest.

Step out with right and again perform block, then step with left up to right foot and perform back fist once more.

Look to front, arms out to side, move your right foot forward, knee in back of right leg, do x block.

Move your left foot back and strongly open your arms.

Step forward into left Junzuki stance and block x, block above your head.

Step into right and perform back fist bringing your left arm up to elbow of right. Twist your body to the right, bring your fist to side of head, bring back performing back fist one more time. Your left arm goes into Gedan-Barai then snaps back into same as 38.

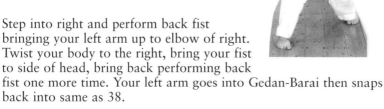

Stepping to your right block left Soto-Uke Jodan your stance is Neko-Ashi, then step and punch Junzuki Chudan.

Twist right and into Neko-Ashi.

Step and punch Junzuki with left arm.

Stepping across to left block Gedan-Barai with right arm.

There is now three Tettsui to face

Right Tettsui

Left Tettsui

K

Side View of 46/47/48

From right Tettsui you are going to step across with left foot into Shiko-Dachi stance.

Right Tettsui

(49)

Right hand on top of left arm below, strike Tettsui to face with left hand, look to your right and place left hand over right and do right Tettusi to face Fig 52.

(50)

(51)

All 49-52 you are in the Shiko-Dachi stance.

(52)

(53)

Bring right foot back to left.

27a
This more sideways move is used by some instructors.

Heisoku-Dachi

36a
Some instructors put this move in between 36/37 of Jion Kata also. Soto-Uke block in Neko-Ashi stance.

Application 49/50

APPLICATIONS

45a

10a

39a

40a

22a

23a

JITTE

Jitte is said to be for disarming a Bo (staff) wielding opponent. Other meanings include Ten Hand or Ten Techniques. The movements at the start are soft but strong, and are very good for strengthening the wrist.

Start with left hand just on right palm (see application).

Step back with left foot into Neko-Ashi (cat stance), your hands in Teisho.

Musubi-Dachi

Stepping to your left, bring your right hand down, your left hand comes upward. Hand still in Teisho, looking to right.

Heisoku-Dachi

Place your left hand on your arm.

Step with right and do Teisho to face, stance Shiko-Dachi.

Whip back your left hand as you twist right hand upwards into Teisho hand.

Some instructors teach 3 Teisho's to face.

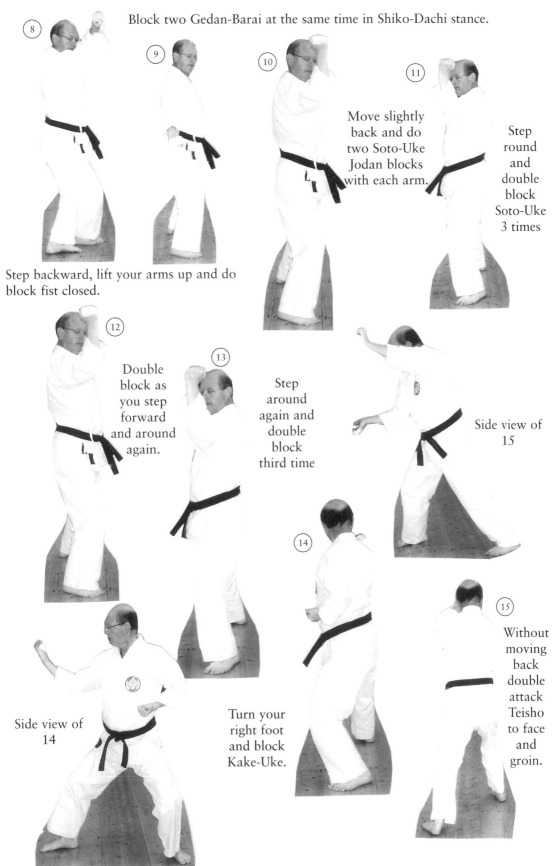

Block two Gedan-Barai at the same time in Shiko-Dachi stance.

Move slightly back and do two Soto-Uke Jodan blocks with each arm.

Step round and double block Soto-Uke 3 times

Step backward, lift your arms up and do block fist closed.

Double block as you step forward and around again.

Step around again and double block third time

Side view of 15

Side view of 14

Turn your right foot and block Kake-Uke.

Without moving back double attack Teisho to face and groin.

Step into left and double block again right Teisho to face left to groin.

Step and perform 15 again, move your back foot across to right.

(16)

(17)

K

(18)

Block same as Pinan Godan to left.

Put weight onto left foot and repeat move to right.

(19)

(20)

(21)

Step block right Jodan-Uke.

Step with left foot forward block, Jodan-Uke (head block)

Step with left to left.

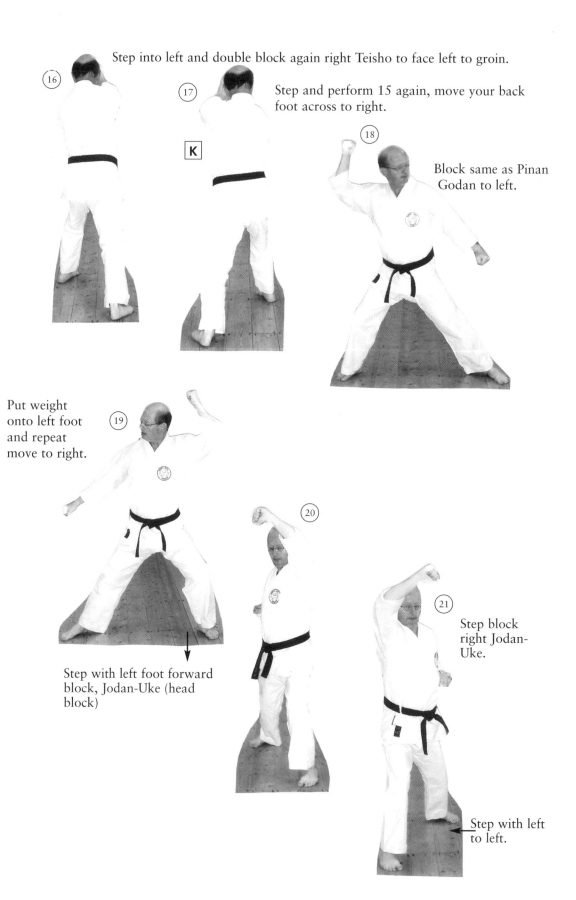

Block left Jodan-Uke.

(22)

Step block right Jodan-Uke

(23)

Turn 180° to left, back into Heisoku-Dachi.

(24)

(25)

Musubi-Dachi

15a

Applications

2a

NISEISHI

I have included two versions of this Kata, the Kata Niseishi history is difficult to trace but the Kata itself is very dynamic and is very popular amongst advanced Karate students.

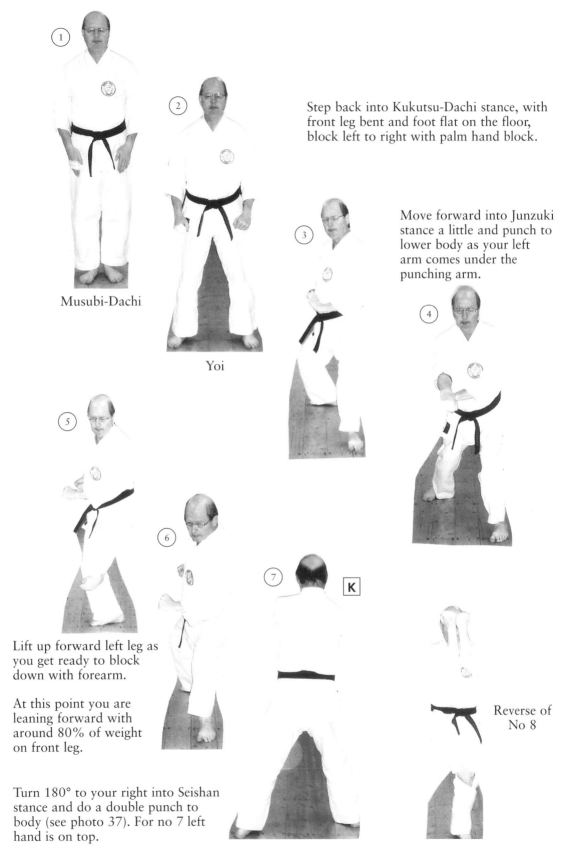

(1)

Musubi-Dachi

(2)

Yoi

(3)

Step back into Kukutsu-Dachi stance, with front leg bent and foot flat on the floor, block left to right with palm hand block.

(4)

Move forward into Junzuki stance a little and punch to lower body as your left arm comes under the punching arm.

(5)

(6)

(7)

K

Reverse of No 8

Lift up forward left leg as you get ready to block down with forearm.

At this point you are leaning forward with around 80% of weight on front leg.

Turn 180° to your right into Seishan stance and do a double punch to body (see photo 37). For no 7 left hand is on top.

209

⑧

Bring your right foot off the ground and at the same time pull both hands back in front of your face (as if protecting them)

Step down into right Junzuki stance, block with your right arm in front of left.

⑨

9a

Reverse of 9

Side view of 8a

9b

Reverse

⑩   Step and Block Jodan-Uke

Move your left foot over a little as you block with right arm. This is same block as performed in Kihon Gumite.

⑪

⑫

Block with side of hand to right using Shuto (side of hand).

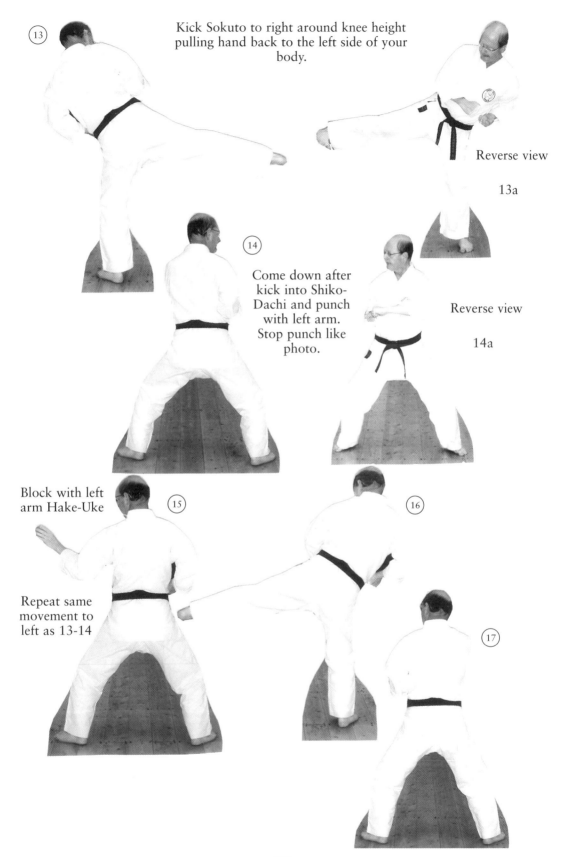

(13) Kick Sokuto to right around knee height pulling hand back to the left side of your body.

Reverse view

13a

(14) Come down after kick into Shiko-Dachi and punch with left arm. Stop punch like photo.

Reverse view

14a

Block with left arm Hake-Uke

(15)

(16)

Repeat same movement to left as 13-14

(17)

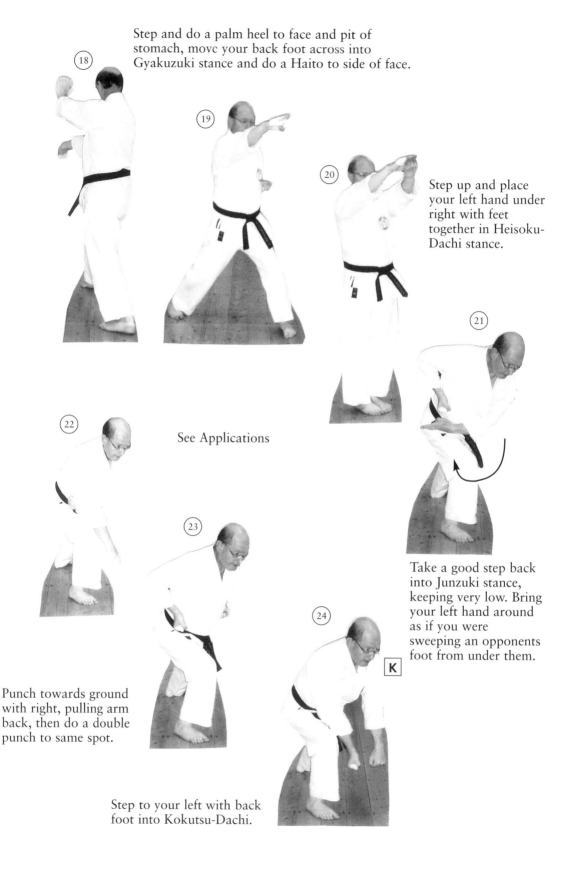

Step and do a palm heel to face and pit of stomach, move your back foot across into Gyakuzuki stance and do a Haito to side of face.

Step up and place your left hand under right with feet together in Heisoku-Dachi stance.

See Applications

Take a good step back into Junzuki stance, keeping very low. Bring your left hand around as if you were sweeping an opponents foot from under them.

Punch towards ground with right, pulling arm back, then do a double punch to same spot.

K

Step to your left with back foot into Kokutsu-Dachi.

212

Block Kake-Uke Chudan (Body) with left hand, stance here is Kokutsu-Dachi with both feet flat on the floor.

Step twisting your body into Shiko-Dachi stance. At same time block like Kihon Kumite, then block down Gedan-Barai.

Block Kake-Uke with left arm stance is Kukutsu-Dachi.

Punch to body stopping like photo with left arm.

Step around and do elbow to body in Shiko-Dachi. Don't move from this stance and block on the spot Gedan-Barai, your non-blocking hand upwards.

213

(32)

Your left foot moves off from photo 30 and blocks Kake-Uke with left arm, stance at this point is Kokutsu-Dachi.

(33)

Step and twist your body into Shiko-Dachi stance, block Kihon Kumite block then bring blocking hand down into Gedan-Barai.

(34)

(35)

Stop punch with left same as photo 28.

(36)

(37) K

Bring your right foot around into Seishan stance using strong tension, pull arm back and double punch right hand on top.

(38)

As you twist arms,
your left foot steps up
to right.

Open hands, twist them left coming up, right going down.
Take them to the side of your body then let your right
hand go up to photo 40. Push both arms out about half
way, the left one toward the groin, the right one towards
the chin.

(39)

(40)

(41)

Stances for 39-41 are
Heisoku-Dachi.

(42)

Yama

(43)

Musubi-Dachi

a

21-24

b

6a

c

Variation Kata 2 No 6a

26a

Using
Kake-Uke
to block.

25a

25b

Then
grab and
punch

19a

41a

NISEISHI 2

Musubi-Dachi

Yoi

Step with left into short Junzuki, block same as first Niseishi.

Open left hand, palm down and punch with right fist.

Lift left foot up

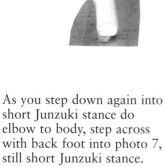

As you step down again into short Junzuki stance do elbow to body, step across with back foot into photo 7, still short Junzuki stance.

Double punch to body, left arm on top (see photo 7a)

K

Side View
7a

(8)

(9) Lift right foot up same as
first Niseishi stepping down
into short Junzuki then
double block.

Side View
9a

(10) Step with your left foot to left
block Jodan-Uke.

(11) Block like Kihon-Kumite, step to
your right into Shiko-Dachi and
perform Kake-Uke.

(12)

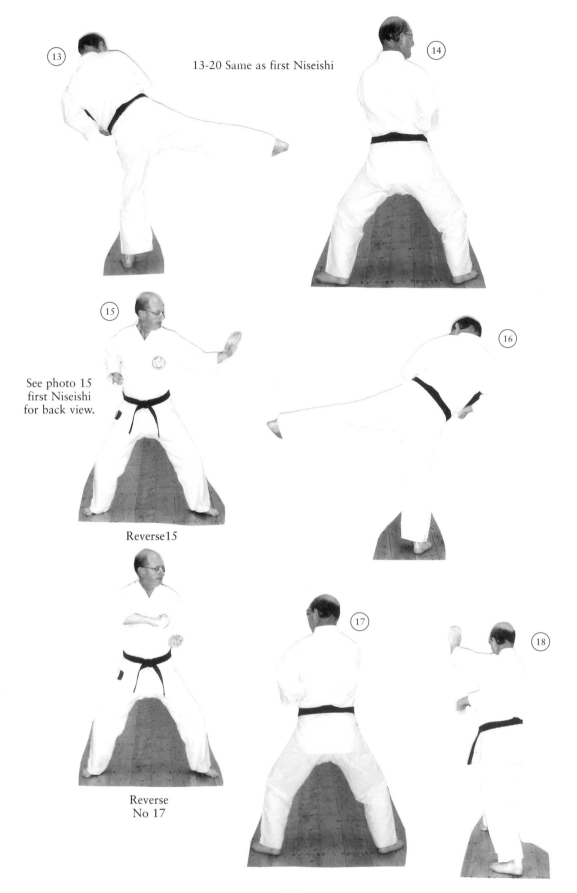

13-20 Same as first Niseishi

See photo 15
first Niseishi
for back view.

Reverse15

Reverse
No 17

19-20 same as Niseishi

22 do palm
heel (Teisho)
at this point

At this point, stance
same as first version

Step to
your
right

K

Step into Tata-Seishan stance, block
with right hand as Kihon Kumite, twist
your body and block Gedan-Barai as
you take up Shiko-Dachi stance.

Move body same as 1st Niseishi with your left foot (no 27) and do 28 same as first Niseishi.

Twist your body back to Tata-Seishan and punch Gyakuzuki.

After elbow angle out the right block.

Back to same movement as 1st Niseishi.

Step and block same as Kihon-Kumite.

Twist body and block Gedan-Barai stance Shiko-Dachi.

Twist body into Gyakuzuki stance Tata-Seishan.

(34)

(35) Turn with right foot into Seishan.

K

(36) Bring arms completely across body as you step up left to right, not making quite as big a circle as first Katas ending.

(37)

(38)

Move left foot only

(39)

Left then right, back to Musubi-Dachi

Application of 6a

WANSHU

Wanshu Kata is said to date back to the 1680s and was introduced into Okinawa by a Chinese envoy. I have included a jump at the end of the Kata, some Wado-Ryu schools don't do this.

1

Musubi-Dachi

2

Start by having your right hand on your left palm.

Heisoku-Dachi

3a - Start stance used by some instructors in Japan.

3b

3

Step out to left, punch down stance Gyakuzuki-no-Tsukkomi.

4

Go into Shiko-Dachi as you look to right, get ready to block.

5

Block Gedan-Barai.

6

Punch, stop punch to body (do not punch past body).

7

Step forward and block Gedan-Barai with left arm stance Junzuki.

Punch Gyakuzuki
on spot

Kick Maegeri

Note:
Photo 9/14/34 some instructors do no kick.

See Application for 10

Move back foot up
to forward leg as you
punch to groin.

Step back into right
Junzuki. Block Gedan-
Barai with right hand.
Step across with back
foot to left.

Block left
Gedan-
Barai

Punch
Gyakuzuki
right arm
to head
(Jodan).

Kick
Maegeri
with right
foot.

10a

Stance and block used by
some instructors in Japan.
Also 15/35 photos.

Bring your left foot up as you do same move as 10-11

(15)

(16)

(17) Step across to
left block left
Gedan-Barai.

Move used by
some instructors
in Japan prior
to 19.

18a

(18)

Rise your left hand then
bring your right hand up to
palm. Your right leg on calf.

(20)

See Application 18/19

(19)

Twist your body
back sharply
into Gyakuzuki-
no-Tsukkomi
and block
Shuto-Uke.

20a
Move
used by
some
instructors
in Japan

(21)

(22)

Twist your body
back into Shiko-
Dachi and punch
right.

Punch left

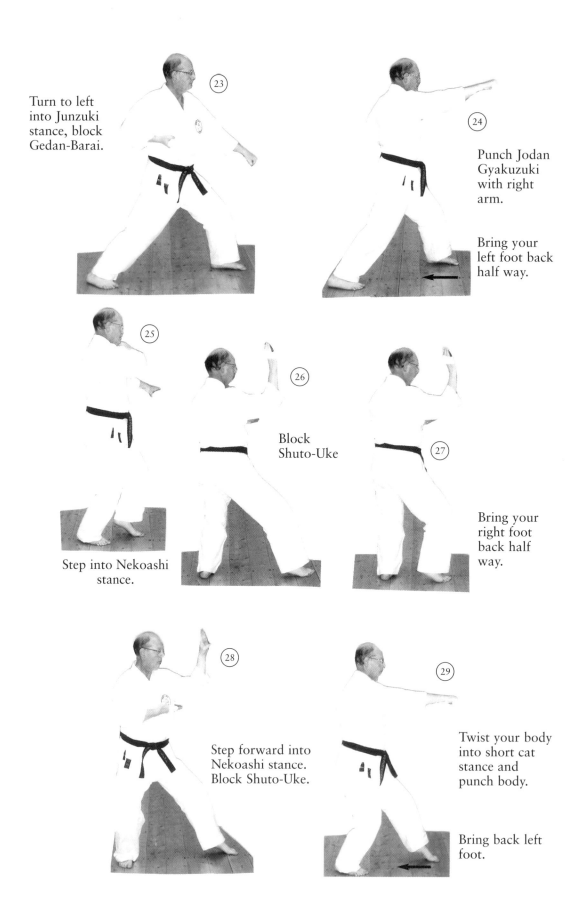

Turn to left into Junzuki stance, block Gedan-Barai.

(23)

(24)

Punch Jodan Gyakuzuki with right arm.

Bring your left foot back half way.

(25)

(26)

Block Shuto-Uke

(27)

Bring your right foot back half way.

Step into Nekoashi stance.

(28)

Step forward into Nekoashi stance. Block Shuto-Uke.

(29)

Twist your body into short cat stance and punch body.

Bring back left foot.

(30) Step forward and block Shuto-Uke with right hand Nekoashi stance.

(31)

(32) Turn to your right and block left Gedan-Barai.

(33) Punch Gyakuzuki Jodan.

K (34) Kick Maegeri

(35)

(35) Step down and do same as photo 10.

Step back and block Gedan-Barai with right arm then step across with left foot to left.

*Note - on 34 you try to get as much momentum forward as you can, this is only for this 3rd one and not for the other two similar movements.

Block left Gedan-Barai.

Twist your body to right, drop your right hand and left hand chin height, both hands in Teisho. Stance at this point is Gyakuzuki-no-Tsukkomi.

Whip your body to your left and do Teisho upwards under chin.

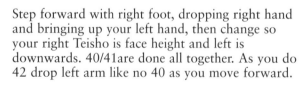

Step forward with right foot, dropping right hand and bringing up your left hand, then change so your right Teisho is face height and left is downwards. 40/41are done all together. As you do 42 drop left arm like no 40 as you move forward.

Step forward into right, back to 41.

Move same leg a little forward and block Gedan-Barai.

K

Jump around into the air, landing in right stance. This is the same movement as Rohai, but in the air.

Move a little forward again and open your hands, one on face, the other on groin.

On landing you are in Shuto-Uke Neko-Ashi stance.

Step back, block into left Shuto-Uke.

Step back into Heisoku-Dachi

Musubi-Dachi

Applications

Punch on foot

3

Block

3a

Dummy with hand

18a

19a

10a

As a block.

10b

Use as a groin punch legs protecting defenders groin.

AUTHOR'S NOTES:

- Yama means the same stance as Yoi, but is used at the end of the Kata.

- Jion Kata also is performed on photos 13-21 in the following order:
    1. Turn left leg forward, head block right arm, head block left arm on the spot. Reverse punch left arm on the spot.

    2. Head block left arm, step forward right leg forward, head block right arm, reverse punch left arm on the spot.

    3. Head block right arm on the spot. Step forward left leg, head block left arm, step forward right leg, punch right arm.

Conclusion

When putting a book together, there is always a problem over what to include and what to leave out. Fortunately Orient-Publishing gave me the opportunity to write four books on Wado-Ryu. This gave me more scope to give the readers a more complete picture of the Art of Wado-Ryu than was ever previously possible.

In Wado-Ryu Fighting Techniques Uncovered I have included Kumite-Gata, Ohyo-Gumite and other fighting techniques and competition sparring. In Wado-Ryu Karate Katas Uncovered I have included many more applications.

I hope you have enjoyed studying this book, and that it helps in spreading the True Art of Wado-Ryu Karate.

Master Hironori Ohtsuka
1892 - 1982

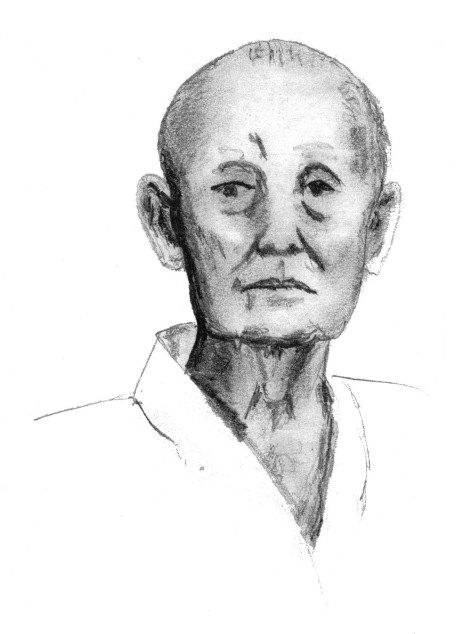

Words of Master Ohtsuka

* * *

Martial arts is not for fighting, but to find your own inner peace!

* * *

Always think for yourself!

* * *

You should do Karate like an old man without tension or effort!

* * *

Practice every day, 30 minutes is better than 4 hours at one time!

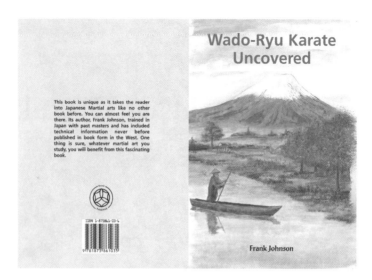

This book is unique as it takes the reader into Japanese Martial arts like no other book before. You can almost feel you are there. Its author, Frank Johnson, trained in Japan with past masters and has included technical information never before published in book form in the West. One thing is sure, whatever martial art you study, you will benefit from this fascinating book.

ISBN 1-873861-03-6

Wado-Ryu Karate Uncovered

Frank Johnson

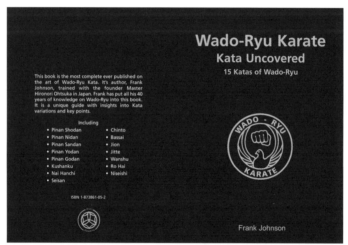

This book is the most complete ever published on the art of Wado-Ryu Kata. It's author, Frank Johnson, trained with the founder Master Hironori Ohtsuka in Japan. Frank has put all his 40 years of knowledge on Wado-Ryu into this book. It is a unique guide with insights into Kata variations and key points.

Including

- Pinan Shodan
- Pinan Nidan
- Pinan Sandan
- Pinan Yodan
- Pinan Godan
- Kushanku
- Nai Hanchi
- Seisan
- Chinto
- Bassai
- Jion
- Jitte
- Wanshu
- Ro Hai
- Niseishi

ISBN 1-873861-05-2

Wado-Ryu Karate
Kata Uncovered
15 Katas of Wado-Ryu

Frank Johnson

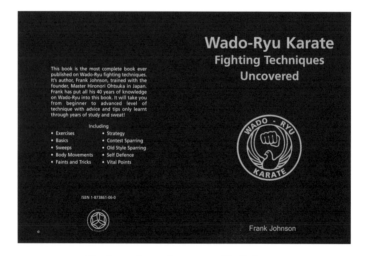

This book is the most complete book ever published on Wado-Ryu fighting techniques. It's author, Frank Johnson, trained with the founder, Master Hironori Ohtsuka in Japan. Frank has put all his 40 years of knowledge on Wado-Ryu into this book. It will take you from beginner to advanced level of technique with advice and tips only learnt through years of study and sweat!

Including

- Exercises
- Basics
- Sweeps
- Body Movements
- Faints and Tricks
- Strategy
- Contest Sparring
- Old Style Sparring
- Self Defence
- Vital Points

ISBN 1-873861-06-0

Wado-Ryu Karate
Fighting Techniques
Uncovered

Frank Johnson

Other books available at
www.orient-publishing.com